D1611090

MAKING SENSE OF CHINDIA

REFLECTIONS ON CHINA AND INDIA

JAIRAM RAMESH

Foreword
STROBE TALBOTT

INDIA RESEARCH PRESS

India Research Press
B-4/22, Safdarjung Enclave, New Delhi – 110 029.
Ph.: 24694610; Fax : 24618637
www.indiaresearchpress.com
bahrisons@vsnl.com ; contact@indiaresearchpress.com

2005

Jairam Ramesh 2005©®India Research Press, New Delhi.

ISBN : 81-87943-95-5

Editorial Assistance & Introductions
Dr. Ravni Thakur, University of Delhi

Cataloguing in Publication Data
Jairam Ramesh
Making Sense of Chindia : Reflections on China and India

1. Security   2. Politics   3. Economy/Economies - India / China.
4. Asia/South Asia. 5. India. 6. China.
        I. Title. II. Author

Printed in India at *Focus Impressions*, New Delhi – 110 003.

Foreword

When my friend Jairam Ramesh sent me the manuscript of this book, I had just completed my third visit to India in the course of a year. There was something almost eerie about how vividly the overarching theme of Jairam's columns collected here resonated with one of my strongest impressions from recent travels to Asia: the change - overwhelmingly for better - in relations between India and China.

That improvement has been even more dramatic for coming about so suddenly. Only seven years ago - in May of 1998 - Former Prime Minister, Atal Bihari Vajpayee, publicly cited the Chinese threat as justification for India's nuclear-weapons test.

China heartily reciprocated Indian animosity. Of the five states whose nuclear-weapons status is recognized by the Non-Proliferation Treaty, China was by far the fiercest in wanting to "punish" India for the Pokhran II test. The Chinese government exuded skepticism about President Bill Clinton's decision to have me enter into a dialogue with Jaswant Singh.

During my diplomatic forays to New Delhi in the two and a half years that followed, I would frequently call on then-Defence Minister George Fernandes, who did nothing to hide a deep personal mistrust of China going back to the early 1960s. And I remember (as I'm sure Chinese officials do as well) one of the most striking passages in an article that Condoleezza Rice, then an adviser to Governor George W. Bush of Texas, wrote in 2000 for Foreign Affairs: she called on the US to improve its relations with India as a counterweight to China, which she and some other members of the Bush team depicted as an emerging strategic competitor to the US.

Fortunately, such thinking in all three countries - India, China and the US - seems to have receded. Returning to New Delhi as a private citizen in early 2003, I found Mr. Fernandes basking in pleasant memories of how well he had been received during an official visit to Beijing. And as the Bush administration begins its second term in office, it seeks to strengthen relations with both India and China each in its own right.

That is the right posture for the United States, since amity between India and China is in the interests of the international community as a whole. Each has opened a closed economy to the world, with the result of booming growth that has benefited vast numbers of its own citizens. But each also suffers from wrenching poverty and disparity. Thus, India and China share another point in common: they have, among their own citizens, both winners and losers in the process of globalization. That Great Divide is potentially the most dangerous source of conflict in the 21st century. If these two dynamic giants, which together are home to a third of humanity, can, within their own borders, close the winner/loser gap and shift the ratio in favor of the winners, it will augur well for all the rest of us.

Jairam has been writing sensibly on this subject for years. It is a mark of his double perspicacity - as journalist and statesman - that he was out in front of one of the more important and promising stories of our era.

Strobe Talbott

February 2005   Brookings Institution, Washington

Contents

Section Three
And Some Other Things

Preface

For long, I have had a scholarly interest in China. Concern with its economy is but natural for somebody like me. But more than that, I have been an amateur student of Chinese history and culture, perhaps because of my fascination with the Buddha and Buddhism. Like most Indians, I grew up learning about Faxian and Xuanzang whose writings have been so very critical to the discovery of our own past. Being a Nehruphile, made me even more conscious of the special links that have always existed between the two cultures, links that have been characterised by mutual borrowing and enrichment.

Casual empiricism is dangerous but to say that a vast majority of Indians are deeply wary of China would not be an exaggeration. The memory of the largely self-imposed debacle in the Himalayas in October/November 1962 still haunts us. Chinese support over the years to insurgent groups in our northeast, its assistance to Pakistan in nuclear and missile technology and its military buildup in the Indian Ocean and the Bay of Bengal have made us even more suspicious. In addition, the prospects of artificially cheap Chinese-made goods driving Indian companies out of business both here and abroad have been unnerving. Our growing bonhomie with the USA has fuelled our sense of rivalry vis-à-vis China further, especially since the new Republican establishment in

Washington lapses into China-phobia ever so frequently.

Although I have instinctive sympathy and appreciation for the "civilisational school" of India-China *wallahs* like P.C. Bagchi, Tan Yun-Shan, Tan Chung and, of recent times, Amartya Sen, I am not a romantic. I am realistic about modern-day China, a China far removed from the days of Kumarajiva and Boddhidharma, two "Indians" who established Buddhism in China in the early part of the first millennium, a China in admiration of India. But my point is that instead of instinctively demonising China as we are prone to do, we must seek to understand it better and also seek to engage it closer across a broad spectrum.

I do not believe that conflict and confrontation is inevitable between the two countries. Yes, there will be competition and sometimes some confrontation perhaps as well, as happened in 1987 at Sumdrung Chu. But that does not make us natural enemies. I also think that not enough Indians give credit to the dramatic changes that are taking place in Chinese society. These changes have heightened interest in India. True, more Indians have written about the India-China connection wistfully than have their Chinese counterparts. It is also true that at one level China sees itself in competition with the USA and feels that it has left India far behind. True, Chinese history books still portray a negative image of India—the land that provided the opium and the police that the British forced down Chinese society in the 19th century and, of course, the land of that bourgeois nationalist Jawaharlal

Nehru which is the only country yet to settle its borders with China. But India's nuclear tests of 1998, its emergence as a major global player in knowledge-based industries like software and pharmaceuticals and the growing clout of the Indian diaspora in the US have fuelled the Chinese desire to know more about India. It is a measure of this interest that there are now more academics in China in its various academies of social sciences specialising on India than is the case vice versa. There is only one Indian journalist representing the Press Trust of India posted full-time in Beijing, while there are at least twelve Chinese journalists working out of New Delhi.

In the past few years, there has been renewed interest in India-China for various reasons. There is the demographic angle with the two accounting for close to two-fifths of the world's population and all that it entails for consumption particularly. There is the growth angle with the two countries being among the fastest growing economies in the world and also being among the four biggest economies according to the purchasing-power parity GDP indicators. There is the strategic angle with the two being declared nuclear powers with a long-festering boundary dispute hanging over them. Ultimately, there is the truth of the next century being propelled by Asia and that is where understanding CHINDIA becomes important.

This is the background to the pieces I wrote in the hope that it will generate interest in the relationship between China and India at more popular levels. I am grateful to Dr. Ravni Thakur who is one of India's most knowledgeable academics on China for having helped put together this collection and giving it a running thread and coherence.

Section One

China vs India to Chindia
Comments on the Geopolitics of the Region

Indian memories of China have been shaped by the events of 1962. Forty-two years on, it is time to leave the past behind and begin afresh. Relations between India and China have improved rapidly since Prime Minister Rajiv Gandhi's visit to China in 1989. Since then, ties between the two countries have been cemented at many levels. Jairam Ramesh, in this section addresses both the security concerns that continue to mediate the otherwise rapidly improving Sino-Indian relationship and brings to the fore issues that may still pose a problem in the future. The author's intent is to specifically focus on the long-term scenario that may emerge between India and China as their economies develop, complement and compete with each other. He has focused on the role of America in the region, how Western scholars perceive the Sino-Indian relationship and China's changing relationship with Pakistan, amongst other issues. He has also analysed the importance of high-level delegations and Prime-Ministerial visits to each country. Here, he delves into the enormously rich relationship that the two countries shared through Buddhism in the ancient period. Based on the author's extensive reading on the subject, this section presents a comprehensive overview of the geopolitics of the region and provides for new ways of looking at old problems. Ultimately, the author agrees with Deng Xiaoping when he says, "intractable issues should be kept aside and progress should be made on other fronts". For India and China, this intractable issue is the long pending border dispute. And here, as the author points out, trust and pragmatism is the key to move forward. Finally, he emphasises how there is no substitute to a peaceful and negotiated settlement of all unsettled inconclusive disputes between the two countries.

The C-I-A Triangle

India and America versus China makes no sense

The "bad guys" in Washington are generally considered to be Donald Rumsfeld, Paul Wolfowitz and their hawkish colleagues at the Pentagon. Colin Powell is widely held to be the champion of the "good guys" club, however miniscule that may be in the Bush-II establishment. Actually, from the Indian point of view, the bad guys are actually the good guys, very India-positive, whereas the General in the State Department is a great champion of the General in Islamabad.

Indo-US military-to-military cooperation has emerged as the one truly outstanding success story of bilateral ties in the past two-three years? Why is the Pentagon so India-friendly? Is it because of our commitment to democracy and diversity? We would like to think it so but that is not the reason. Is it because of our economic performance and potential? Could be, but only to a very limited extent. The underlying rationale for India looming large on the Pentagon radar screen is China. American conservatives see India as a crucial ally in US policy of China-containment, a sentiment that echoes favourably among large sections of the Indian ruling elite as well. In some senses, there is nothing new in this approach. After all, in the early 1950s, massive American aid to India found many advocates in Washington so as to push democratic India ahead of Communist China. Now, the motivation is not economic—barring a few areas like software exports, China is far ahead of India. China has also integrated itself far closer than India into the US economy—the volume of bilateral Sino-US trade is, for instance, over six times that of Indo-US trade, both merchandise and services. Instead, geopolitics is the new driving force.

A few days ago, the US Secretary of Defence received a classified 130-page document prepared by his analysts called *Indo-US Military Relationship: Expectations and Perceptions.* This report has been made available to the influential Jane's Foreign Report which carried excerpts very recently. The analysis is based largely on interviews with 82 senior Indian and American officials, 50 of whom are military officers, both retired and on active duty. The conclusion is blunt: "China represents the most significant threat to both countries' security in the future as an economic and military competitor". One US officer is quoted as saying: "We want a friend in 2020 that will be capable of assisting the US militarily to deal with a Chinese threat". Indian sources are quoted as having pointed to the reality of China supplying nuclear and missile technology to Pakistan, weapons to Bangladesh, making deep inroads into Myanmar, building the deep-water Gwadar port in Baluchistan and resuming the supply of arms to various insurgent groups in the northeast.

The Pentagon report comes close on the heels of John

Garver's *The China-India-US Triangle: Strategic Relations in the Post-Cold War Era* that was published some six months ago by the Seattle-based National Bureau of Asian Research. Garver who teaches at Atlanta's Georgia Institute of Technology is America's foremost academic on India-China in a comparative strategic perspective. Two years ago, his book *Protracted Contest: Sino-Indian Rivalry in the 20ʰ Century,* a work of meticulous analysis and formidable scholarship. Garver's belief is that India and China share a fundamentally antagonistic and competitive relationship in which conflict is inherent. According to him, "Rather than allowing the new Sino-Indian-US triangle to evolve towards an ever-shifting, flexible, three-cornered minuet, continuation of Beijing's abrasive policies of the 1990s may well move the new triangle in the direction of a fairly stable combination of India and the United States against China". Forging a new India-US relationship will, he says, "have triangular consequences regardless of US intentions".

There are many in this country who will undoubtedly welcome a Washington-New Delhi informal axis to "spook and unsettle" Beijing, if not create "shock and awe". But thanks largely to the pragmatism of Chinese leaders who suggested that the boundary dispute be set aside to foster an economic relationship, there has been a dramatic upsurge in commercial links between India and China. During January-December 2002, two-way trade amounted to $4.9 billion. If Taiwan and Hong Kong are also included, this figure is close to $9 billion, and in 2004 touched the ten billion mark, not all that critical for "Greater" China no doubt, but almost a tenth of India's international trade volume. China's entry into the WTO is opening numerous market opportunities for India. Now that the bogey of Chinese goods swamping India has been buried, Indian companies too are shedding their diffidence and fear. Companies like Ranbaxy, Tisco, SAIL, Bharat Forge, JK Tyres, NIIT, Essel Packaging and TCS already have a growing presence in Chinese markets and TCS is on the final shortlist of three for the prestigious computerisation of the Shanghai Stock Exchange. Other firms like Sundram Fasteners, Apollo Tyres, Samtel, Asian Paints and Infosys will soon make their presence felt. Our foreign office is, no doubt, wary of China and in January 2003 Mr. Jaswant Singh set diplomacy aside and pooh-poohed Chinese statistics. The Chinese feel that India is being unnecessarily obstructive in the matter of granting business visas and in approving Chinese FDI and contracts won in public tenders. The Chinese networking major Huawei Technologies has a sizeable presence in Bangalore and wants to expand, much to the discomfiture of Indian security agencies.

There is simply no substitute for dialogue between the two Himalayan neighbours tied together by their common legacies spawned by Buddhism. This interaction has to be sustained at many levels—political, military, academic, media, sports, culture, etc. Sub-regional cooperation involving, for example, India's northeast, Bangladesh, Myanmar and China's Yunnan Province has great potential—but while others are keen, official Delhi is suspicious. To be sure, we have differences on a whole host of regional issues.

A permanent boundary agreement, that must necessarily involve both India and China giving up territory, is a distant prospect. China's ties with Pakistan have a logic, disturbing as it may be, of their own that we are unable to appreciate. India cannot dilute its relationship with the Dalai Lama, just as it encourages a direct Sino-Tibetan dialogue and as it hopes that eventually he would return to Tibet to a life of dignity, safety and freedom. Even so, we cannot allow ourselves to be mesmerised by the Americans and their encomiums to us in the hope that we will be an ally in their China policy that has a definite adversarial basis. We must continue to engage the US intensively and extensively—and in this, we have to learn much from China. But this should not be at the cost of a deeper relationship with China. Without being romantic, we can still be realistic. As a nation, we have to invest more in creating the intellectual capital to understand and deal with China more effectively. India's acquiring "big power" status on the world stage depends critically on this, apart from making peace with Pakistan—and the two are not unrelated.

The India-China Formula

99.9% Good, 0.1% Bad

Braving SARS and by sticking to his scheduled visit when travel to China is being shunned, the irrepressible Mr. George Fernandes has lived up to his daredevil reputation. In the process, he has also imparted a whole new dimension to Sino-Indian ties. In his professional capacity, Mr. Fernandes is head of our defence establishment that is deeply suspicious of China. In his personal capacity, he has been an ardent champion of the Tibetan cause. That such a personality could have had such a successful visit bodes well for both countries.

Actually, it is not much of a surprise if only we care to appreciate the nuanced change in China's stance on many issues. In December 1996 that President Jiang Zemin most unexpectedly told his Pakistani hosts that India and Pakistan must set aside their differences and foster an economic relationship. During the Kargil war, the Chinese stance was a tacit acceptance of the LOC in Jammu and Kashmir as the international border.

The Chinese are great empiricists. In the early 1980s, Deng Xiaoping observed that Mao was 70% right and 30% wrong. Such an honest assessment of icons in public is simply unthinkable in India. Now, the new Chinese Prime Minister Wen Jiabao has given us some new numbers to think about. On April 21ˢᵗ while speaking to Mr. Fernandes , he noted that "during the past 2200 years, or about 99.9% of the time, we have devoted to friendly cooperation between our two countries". Indeed so.

Obviously, 1962 accounts for the overwhelming bulk of the missing 0.1% in Wen Jiabao's historical arithmetic. But it has cast a disproportionately long shadow. We cling to the idea that India was attacked. Neville Maxwell in his *India's China War* held us primarily responsible for the border war. He was vilified in this country, although privately his views have considerably greater support amongst Indian scholars and experts. An IFS luminary who was liaison officer to Zhou Enlai during that Chinese Premier's ill-fated visit to New Delhi in April 1960 bemoans that India blew a great opportunity of settling the border question at a time when the Chinese were also keen to close the issue. Sections of the Congress Party along with Opposition MPs like Atal Bihari Vajpayee sabotaged Jawaharlal Nehru. It is poetic justice that BJP MPs are doing to Mr. Vajpayee on Pakistan what Mr. Vajpayee himself did to Panditji on China by speeches that were long on emotion and eloquence but short on substance and facts.

Some scholars, however, locate the roots of the 1962 conflict in domestic Chinese upheavals. In his monumental *The Origins of the Cultural Revolution*, Roderick Macfarquhar, the distinguished India-born Sinologist who teaches at Harvard, has called the 1962 battle Mao's India War. The truth is complex. Dr.

Sarvepalli Gopal whose first death anniversary fell recently and who, along with Jagat Mehta, was responsible for formulating India's case on the border issue laughingly admitted before his death that had he been engaged by the Chinese as an independent expert, he could well have made out an equally valid and strong claim on their behalf. Three years ago, two retired IFS officers and China experts C.V.Ranganathan and Vinod Khanna offered such a balanced perspective on the emotive border issue in their *India and China: The Way Ahead* that remains the most incisive and constructive work on this subject. Their conclusion: both sides have to give up territory and they must prepare their public for this inevitability.

A small fraction of the troublesome 0.1% that Wen Jiabao implied must surely be the period immediately following the May 1998 nuclear tests by India. In a most perplexing move, Mr. Atal Bihari Vajpayee wrote to President Bill Clinton pointing to China as the reason for India going nuclear. The letter became public. Soon thereafter, Mr. Fernandes himself was widely quoted as having said that China is India's enemy number one. He has, however, consistently denied ever having made such a statement. Fortunately, the damage by both the Clinton letter and Fernandes's purported statement was contained quickly. A measure of our maturity in handling the situation is reflected in the fact that Mr. Vajpayee's government having earned a Sinophobic image steadfastly refused to heed the protectionist pleas of Indian industry that raised the bogey of Chinese goods swamping Indian markets. Over the past two-three years in a remarkable turnaround, large segments of Indian industry have developed self-confidence to compete with China both in India and elsewhere including in China itself.

While the two countries keep meeting to resolve the boundary question on the basis of landmark agreements signed in 1993 and 1996 and while the economic relationship expands, new scholarship keeps emerging to give contemporary meaning to Wen Jiabao's statement. The works of Chinese scholars such as Xinriu Liu and Wang Bangwei have greatly enhanced our knowledge of the cultural contacts between India and China. A little over a decade ago, Tan Chung, the well-known Indian scholar of Chinese ancestry whose father set up the Cheena Bhavan at Santiniketan, brought, for the Indira Gandhi National Centre for the Arts, a comprehensive volume called *Across the Himalayan Gap* that had described in detail the multifaceted relationship between the two ancient civilisations. Then came Louise Levathes's *When China Ruled the Seas,* that looked at the colourful Admiral Zheng He's voyages to the Malabar coast in the very early 15ᵗʰ century. Subsequently, *The Unknown Hsuan-Tsang,* by the reputed historian Devahuti, author of an earlier classic on Harsha, appeared.

A couple of months ago, as part of the Project of History of Indian Science, Philosophy and Culture that is directed by Professor D.P. Chattopadhyaya, a magisterial volume *India's Interaction with China, Central and West Asia* edited by A. Rahman was released. And just a few days ago, Tansen Sen's absolutely fascinating *Buddhism, Diplomacy and Trade* appeared in which he challenges conventional wisdom and meticulously explores the realignment of Sino-Indian relations during 600-1400, a period which saw the demise of Buddhism in India and its appropriation by the Chinese and other East Asians, a period in which Islamic networks supplanted earlier Buddhist networks and also a period in which regional maritime trade pivoted around the Cholas' expansion leading to the spread of Hinduism in east and southeast China. Incidentally, this brilliant 35-year-old historian, who grew up and studied in Beijing, married a Chinese and now teaches in New York, is the son of N.C. Sen, himself a noted China scholar now retired in Kolkata.

Jiang Zemin now the chairman of the Central Military Commission broke all protocol while greeting Mr. Fernandes. He joked that he likes meeting young people and since Mr. Fernandes is four years younger, he was very pleased to spend time with him. Jiang Zemin went on to add that since Mr. Vajpayee is three or four months younger than him, he is eagerly looking forward to the Indian Prime Minister's visit. The momentum and atmospherics generated by Mr. Fernandes's landmark trip should not be lost. One immediate offshoot should be greater support to Indian academics working on the 2200 years of Sino-Indian interactions that remain largely unexplored and that Wen Jiabao recalled in a Nehruvian fashion.

15

Vajpayee Goes to China

Time for bold new bilateral and regional initiatives

In a departure from usual protocol, the Defence Minister, Mr. George Fernandes, has announced that Mr. Atal Bihari Vajpayee will visit China next month. Mr. Vajpayee's delayed visit during these troubled times of SARS will undoubtedly be appreciated by the Chinese who have had to see the cancellation of several travel plans including that of the US Vice-President Dick Cheney and of the Singapore Prime Minister Goh Chok Tong.

Mr. Vajpayee's will be the fourth prime ministerial visit in the last 50 years. Jawaharlal Nehru received a very warm welcome in October 1954 and the detailed record of his wide-ranging discussions with Mao and Zhou Enlai contained in the *Selected Works of Jawaharlal Nehru (Second Series, Volume 27)* make fascinating reading even today. After the long chill following the 1962 war, it was Indira Gandhi who began the process of normalisation of bilateral relations on January 1, 1969 by a statement that "the Indian government would be prepared to try for ways of solving conflicts with China through talks that are not based on any pre-conditions". However, she was unable to go the full distance. Rajiv Gandhi's visit of December 1988 transformed the bilateral relationship. P.V. Narasimha Rao visited China in 1993. It was under his leadership that the landmark "Agreement on the Maintenance of Peace and Tranquillity Along the Line of Actual Control in the India-China Border Areas" was signed in Beijing in September 1993. This was followed up by another historic "Agreement on confidence-building measures in the military field along the line of actual control in the India-China border areas" that was signed in November 1996.

Mr. Vajpayee himself first went to China as External Affairs Minister in February 1979 and met Deng Xiaoping himself. This Vajpayee visit was indeed a breakthrough in a number of areas although it was to be overshadowed by China's attack on Vietnam that led him to cut short his visit. Mr. Vajpayee would undoubtedly be accompanied by his Principal Secretary Brajesh Mishra. There is some history here too. Mr. Mishra was the Indian Charge d'Affaires in Beijing when on May 1, 1970 Mao, perhaps in response to Indira Gandhi's earlier statement, turned to him at the podium of Tiananmen Square and said, "India is a great country and the Indian people are a great people. Chinese and Indian people ought to live as friends, they cannot always quarrel".

Mr. Vajpayee's visit is taking place when bilateral trade is galloping. But this two-way trade amounting to about $10 billion in 2004, is still more critical to India than it is to China. That asymmetry has to be changed. Indian business has developed a great deal of self-confidence vis-à-vis China. Corporate morale was low five years ago but today the picture is completely different.

Mr. Vajpayee will do well to take a strong business delegation with him. This would also give an impetus to the first-ever "Made in India" show that the Confederation of Engineering Industry is organising in October 2003 in Beijing. He would also do well to allay doubts that have arisen in the minds of the Chinese that the Indian government—not Indian companies—is suspicious of Chinese investments in India. We have debarred a leading Hong Kong-based company from bidding for a port project in Nhava Sheva on grounds of security. Chinese investments in states like Himachal Pradesh is discouraged. We are worried that a Hong Kong-based multinational is now the leading mobile telephone company in India. We have been very wary of the expansion plans of Chinese telecom major Huawei which already employs over 500 Indian engineers in Bangalore and also of the Chinese consumer goods giant Haier. There is also frustration in China on delays on the Indian side in granting visas. With proper papers, you can get a visa in Delhi to go to China in about three-four days while it can take two-three weeks to get an Indian visa in Beijing.

The Chinese would undoubtedly have taken note of Mr. Vajpayee's statement in Parliament on May 8th to the effect that while Pakistan's nuclear programme is India-centric, India's nuclear programme is based on threats from other countries in the region. There is nothing new in this formulation. But it is clearly time to do something about it. Our approach to nuclear issues has been global. While this is laudable, we must explore regional options as well. A trilateral confidence-building non-proliferation initiative involving India, China and Pakistan is in our interest. Such an initiative could well be kickstarted through a non-official Track II that has yielded such good results on the Indo-American front. There are other regional bodies like the six-nation Shanghai Cooperation Organisation that are of great interest to India. Energy linkages with the Tarim Basin Asia could usefully be explored in an Eurasian framework. The "Kunming Initiative" involving India, China, Bangladesh and Myanmar that envisages land connectivity, trade and mutual investments is particularly significant for our northeast.

Although the Indo-US economic relationship is not as dynamic and spectacular like the Sino-US economic relationship, Indo-US military ties have grown impressively in the last two years with many high-level exchanges of defence officers, joint army, air force and navy exercises, cooperation in training and procurement. The Chinese have watched warily. The challenge for us is to convey in as clear a fashion that deepening military collaboration with the USA is not directed against China in any way even if Washington sees the rise of Chinese power as one of its three most crucial strategic concerns, next only to the rise of Islamic fundamentalism and the spread of weapons of mass destruction.

Mr. Vajpayee will also be going to Beijing at an unusual moment of time when there is a parallelism or even coincidence of Chinese and American interests vis-à-vis the subcontinent. These include the promotion of an Indo-Pak dialogue, curbing proliferation of nuclear weapons, destroying terrorist networks and support for Pakistan's economic development as a modern, secular nation. This opens up new opportunities for us to try and manoeuvre an increased understanding of India's positions in relation to Pakistan with Chinese interlocutors. China's policy in the subcontinent has become more nuanced, nuclear and missile sales to Pakistan notwithstanding. China will not abandon Pakistan nor will the USA— indeed, a constructive US-China-Pakistan triangle could well be in our interest. That apart, our position on Pakistan would get a great boost in China if we are seen to be expediting movement leading to mutual agreement on the line of actual control along the Sino-Indian border. More imaginative use could be made of the existing 1993 and 1996 Agreements to arrive at a delineation of the line of actual control without prejudice to the positions of the two sides on the contentious boundary question.

A new economic China is manifest. But a new political China is also emerging. Alas, most Indian are trapped in the old mindsets and are unable to see the profound implications of the transitions that have taken place across the Himalayas.

The Rediscovery of Nehru

*The Prime Minister shows
political vision and courage in Beijing*

What an extraordinary coincidence that just as the 50th
anniversary of Shyama Prasad Mukherjee's death fell, Atal
Bihari Vajpayee was rediscovering Jawaharlal Nehru in
Beijing. The irony could not be greater for Mr. Vajpayee
was among the Indians who had made it virtually
impossible for Panditji to accept Zhou Enlai's "package
deal" for the permanent solution of the border dispute
during 1958-60. Domestic critics will undoubtedly vilify
the Prime Minister for a "sell out" and for getting only
"implicit" concessions from the Chinese in return for our
"explicit" compromises. These fears are groundless and are
based on a lack of appreciation of the nuanced and
measured manner in which the Chinese conduct their
foreign policy.

While ultimately the Prime Minister himself deserves the
kudos for the political direction he has charted, some of
his aides have played a key role in facilitating this
conceptual breakthrough. First, Brajesh Mishra himself
who was the recipient of Mao's ice-breaking homily of
May 1, 1970 that " India is a great country and the Indian
people are a great people. Chinese and Indian people ought

to live as friends, they cannot always quarrel". And second the outgoing Indian Ambassador in Beijing Shiv Shankar Menon who appears to have China running through his system. Not only has he been a student of Chinese history and a China-specialist but he is also the grandson of the redoubtable K.P.S. Menon who was our Agent-General and Ambassador in China during 1943-47, the nephew of another K.P.S. Menon who was Foreign Secretary at the time of Rajiv Gandhi's truly historic December 1988 trip to China and the son-in-law of R.D. Sathe who had served in Kashgar and later been our Ambassador in Beijing in the very late 1970s.!

Mr. Vajpayee's trip has received headlines for its very strong economic component. Trade is all set to expand even further while a new beginning is on the anvil for investment ties. Hopefully, the Prime Minister's vision will overcome the suspicion that still exists here to the growing Chinese presence in India. Unlike his meetings with other world leaders, the subject of terrorism appears to have been overshadowed in his talks with Chinese leaders. It may well have come up for the Chinese are indeed worried by what is happening particularly in the northwestern province of Xinjiang. It is because of links between the Taliban and Islamic separatist groups in Xinjiang that China sought to buy peace with Mullah Omar's regime. And it is certainly one reason why China would like to maintain more than cordial ties with Pakistan.

Indeed, the concern over the three "isms"—terrorism,

24

extremism and separatism - is also one of the main reasons why the Chinese have taken the initiative to establish the Shanghai Cooperation Organisation (SCO) by roping in Russia, Kazakhistan, Uzbekistan, Kyrgyzistan and Tajikistan. The SCO is meant to promote regional security and economic integration. While the secretariat is in China, a regional anti-terrorism agency has come into being in the Kyrgyz capital of Bishkek. While, the SCO was conceived of prior to the events of September 11, 2001 and therefore had something of an anti-American flavour, the establishment of an American presence in Afghanistan and Central Asia and the growing bonhomie between Russia and America in the wake of 9/11 has given it a whole new orientation.

The Chinese accord great importance to the SCO and see it both as a means of fostering closer ties with Russia and also as a means of expanding their influence in Central Asia. Central Asia is important to China economically as, according to present trends, China will soon be importing between a third and two-fifth of its oil requirements. There has been some talk of India joining the SCO but not much progress has been made. The Russians have been particularly keen on our entry. Pakistan, Iran, Mongolia and Sri Lanka have also expressed an interest in joining the organisation.

September 11 evoked world-wide interest in Islam. Islam is not normally associated with China, as it is with India or Indonesia but it has played a significant role in

25

Chinese history. Beginning in the 10th century, Muslim traders played a significant role in globalising China's economy. They filled the gap caused by the demise of Indian Buddhism and promoted Sino-Indian trade. The famous Chinese explorer Admiral Zheng He, who made several epochal voyages in the first two decades of the fifteen century including to the Malabar Coast was a Muslim. But denigration of Islam, as the eminent anthropologist Dru Gladney points out in his classic *Muslim Chinese* has had a long and respectable history in China. This has persisted into modern times and in the immediate aftermath of the founding of the People's Republic of China in 1949 there was a major suppression of Islam. As late as during the Cultural Revolution the Weizhou Great Mosque in northern China described as the most beautiful mosque in China was destroyed. But since then, attitudes have begun to change and Muslims are getting increasing political, economic and cultural space. Muslim students have indulged in public protests like in 1989, as observed by Gladney, against the publication of a book in Chinese called *Xing Fengsu* or *Sexual Customs*, a book akin to Salman Rushdie's *Satanic Verses*.

Estimates vary but the official count is that today about 2% of China is Muslim—that is, China has around 20 million Muslims. Xinjiang has been a Muslim-majority province but in typical Chinese style, the demographics have been altered as it has been in Tibet by mass resettlement of the dominant Han communities. Over the past four decades, the Han proportion of Xinjiang's population has increased to at least 40%. Xinjiang's population is just 18-20 million but its importance lies in its natural resources like hydrocarbons and minerals and in the fact that it covers a sixth of China's land area. Pipelines to bring in Xinjiang's enormous reserves of oil and gas into the eastern region are being planned. The Uygur of Xinjiang are one of the ten so-called Muslim nationalities of China, the others being the Hui, Kazak, Dongxiang, Kyrgyz, Salar, Tajik, Uzbek. Baoan and Tatar. The Hui are the most numerous and are found all over China but especially in the provinces of Ningxia, Gansu, Henan, Xinjiang, Qinghai, Yunnan and Hebei. The northern province of Ningxia is an autonomous region even though the Han constitute the vast majority there. While Uygur activism and the East Turkestan Islamic Movement (ETIM) continues to receive international attention, much less is known about other revivalist groups like the Salaffiya that seem to be growing in China.

China's rich Buddhist legacy, which Mr. Vajpayee will see in Luoyang, continues to be the subject of new scholarship. We may exult in this, although the Chinese have Sinified Buddhism evidenced, for instance, by the transformation of the male Avalokitesvara into the female Guanyin. But it is China's not inconsiderable Islamic heritage that will impart an additional dimension to Sino-Indian political ties. In addition, the presence of Sanskritic and Tamil culture in southeast China particularly is something waiting to be explored more systematically.

27

Hopefully, the new chapter that Mr. Vajpayee's visit has opened will intensify deeper cross-cultural understanding as well.

No Space Race Please

China scores big but there is no need for India to feel defensive or threatened

The Chinese space programme clearly has been a spectacular success. It has enhanced China's international stature and given it entry into an elite club of countries that have put humans in space and that has hitherto consisted of just the USA and Russia. The temptation to emulate what China has done is always irresistible in this country. After China's very recent achievement, the pressure on us, self-imposed entirely, will be very great. Plans for sending an unmanned spacecraft to the moon by 2006/07 have been announced and the Prime Minister has gone one step further and given Kennedy-like expression to the dream of an Indian on the moon in a decade's time. It would be a disaster if we fell into this "me too" race. There is simply no need to feel defensive about our own space programme. This has been an outstanding technological and managerial accomplishment and has had tremendous developmental impacts in diverse fields. These have to be sustained and expanded, not frittered away in the pursuit of some false sense of national pride and prestige.

China's space programme has always been and continues to be military-driven. The story of how and why the military came to play such a pivotal role in the country's scientific and technological development has just been unravelled in Evan Feigenbaum's brilliant new book *China's Techo-Warriors*. Like its nuclear weapons programme as described in the classic *China Builds the Bomb* by John Wilson Lewis and Xue Litai, China's space programme was established in the background of the Korean War (1950-53), the Taiwan Straits crisis (1954-55) and of unfolding events in Indochina in the early 50s. It received the initial impetus from the USSR but this assistance ended by 1960. While Mao provided the political leadership, it was Marshal Nie Rongzhen who is today acknowledged as the father of the space programme. Others like Liu Bocheng and Peng Dehuai also provided the military thrust.

It was actually Qian Xuesen who laid the scientific and technological foundations of China's space programme. Ironically, in the midst of the McCarthy hysteria that had gripped the USA in the mid-1950s, Qian was expelled from the USA in 1955 after staying and prospering in that country for twenty years. Before that, he was a highly distinguished member of the faculty of the prestigious California Institute of Technology (Caltech) at Pasadena where he was a co-founder of the famous Jet Propulsion Laboratory. Qian who was a rocket specialist with several theoretical contributions still standing to his name, had also served in the US army. Other key scientific figures in the early years included Yang Jiachi who had studied at Harvard University, Ren

Xinmin who had studied at the University of Michigan, Wang Daheng who was England-educated and Chen Fangyun who had worked in England in the late 1940s. "Purely" local products who played a crucial role in establishing the space programme included Huang Weilu and Li Xu'e.

Cambridge-educated Vikram Sarabhai provided the original vision to India's space programme in the late 1960s. But he died prematurely in 1971. Thereafter, Satish Dhawan imbued with the same vision gave shape to Sarabhai's legacy and took the space programme to new heights of technological achievements never forgetting Sarabhai's fundamental objective- space for developmental applications like telecommunications, broadcasting, meteorology and resource management. Indira Gandhi who could very easily have used the space programme for national "prestige" or for political purposes agreed wholeheartedly with the Sarabhai-Dhawan focus on the essentiality of creating not an Indian *Space* Research Organisation but an *Indian* Space Research Organisation. The only "diversion" for ISRO came in the mid-1980s with the joint Indo-Soviet enterprise that put Squadron Leader Rakesh Sharma into orbit. But fortunately that was only momentary and did not cost ISRO anything. It was Dhawan who kept India's space programme a wholly civilian enterprise, an enterprise derived from and intimately linked to the social and economic needs and requirements of the country. While other noted scientists and technologists of his generation spent their time in

31

political *parikramas* in New Delhi, Dhawan never moved out of Bangalore, insulated ISRO from political and bureaucratic interference and enhanced the institutional character and strength of ISRO by the manner in which he conducted himself in retirement.

It is an interesting coincidence that like Qian, Satish Dhawan also took his doctorate from Caltech in 1951. These two giants of their respective countries must have known and interacted with each other in the small, exclusive setting of Caltech. Their largely similar political beliefs would have drawn them even closer together. Dhawan shunned the media and hence he is not a household name. But he was indeed a most unusual personality, having an undergraduate degree in physics and mathematics, a masters in English literature, another undergraduate degree in mechanical engineering, a post-graduate degree in aeronautical engineering and a doctorate in aeronautical engineering and mathematics. He was, as Roddam Narasimha put it in his obituary article that appeared in *Current Science*, India's first engineering scientist.

The fact that China's space programme has been military-oriented has undoubtedly given it a clear edge in launch vehicle technology. Incidentally, China's launch site is in the northwest Gansu province not very far from Dunhuang at the edge of the Gobi Desert, a city that lay on a crucial junction of the Silk Road and the site of the extraordinary Mogao caves discovered just over a century ago that housed a fabulous collection of Buddhist literature, paintings, sculptures, textiles and other priceless relics. But in almost all scientific and engineering aspects of satellite technology barring the military satellite area, India is clearly ahead even though the Chinese have launched more satellites than India has (around 50 as compared to 35). It is generally not known that while China's space programme started a good decade and a half earlier than India's, India had very quickly narrowed the time gap. China launched its first satellite in 1970, while India did so in 1975. The momentum has been maintained. This Indian leadership in satellite technology is acknowledged by the Chinese themselves. A whole slew of satellites are scheduled to be put in orbit by India in the next few years. These cover not just the traditional areas of communications, broadcasting, weather forecasting and remote sensing but in other areas like education, distance learning, disaster management and telemedicine as well.

China's unmanned and manned space flight programme was launched in the late 1970s although its existence was publicly revealed and confirmed only much later. And in the 1990s, China gained significantly from cooperation with a Russia desperate for hard currency. That route may also be available to India. But a space flight programme would just divert managerial resources and attention away from satellite design, launch and use. A one-off unmanned space flight may not quite be a disaster and could well have some economic spin-offs. But whether it can remain "one-off" is a moot point. It is time-consuming. But more than that, as the Americans discovered to their cost, one flight leads to another and before you know it, you are caught in a trap of technonationalism that generates a lot of euphoria all-round but whose enduring value is dubious.

New CPI Equations

China's high-pressure, low-profile role in pushing Pakistan to talk to India

Bonhomie between India and Pakistan is in the air yet again. Somewhat unexpectedly, the rhetoric emanating from Islamabad is subdued, moderate and even statesmanlike. Many believe that American pressure is finally paying off and that Pakistan is, at last, beginning to fall in line to the dictates of the Bush administration. But could there be other pressures on General Musharraf as well? Evidence is accumulating that China too has, in its own way, told Pakistan "enough is enough", that it should crack down on its sponsorship of export-oriented terrorist outfits and that it should open a dialogue with India. Based on high-level background briefings in all three countries, *The Asian Wall Street Journal* highlighted the Chinese role in the new opening between Islamabad and New Delhi. The following quote from the article of December 8th is significant.

"Chinese leaders advised President Musharraf to be forward-looking and to respond positively" to India's latest overture, says a Pakistani official who made the trip. This official says the Chinese were visibly irritated when Mr. Musharraf raised the issue of China's growing business ties with India. "We had decided some 25 years ago to concentrate on economic development," one Chinese official told Mr. Musharraf, according to the Pakistani official, implying that Pakistan should do the same".

Why have the Chinese changed? It is true that in both the 1965 and 1971 Indo-Pak wars, China's support to Pakistan consisted largely of rhetoric. But China played an important role in building up Pakistan's nuclear and missile capability particularly in the 1980s. China and Pakistan share a warm relationship with the Chinese never having forgotten the pivotal role played by Pakistan in re-establishing Sino-US ties in 1971-72. For a while in the 80s as it was re-emerging on the world scene, China also used Pakistan as a bridgehead to the oil-rich Middle East, especially to Saudi Arabia and Iran. But in spite of the close friendship, things have begun to change.

The first evidence for this was provided on December 2, 1996 when President Jiang Zemin addressed the Pakistani Senate and said, "if certain issues cannot be resolved for the time being, they may be shelved temporarily so that they will not affect the normal state-to-state relations". The reference to Kashmir was unmistakable. The Chinese President's spokesman later elaborated on China's position on J&K even more directly and explicitly thus: "China's consistent policy is that the issue should be solved through peaceful consultations. It should be settled by these two countries (that is, India and Pakistan). Our position remains unchanged and the issue (that is, of Kashmir) should be settled through peaceful means. It is a problem left over from history. Pakistan and India have some differences. Kashmir is a very complicated and sensitive issue".

Thereafter, during the Kargil War of 1999 in many ways a defining moment in Sino-Pak ties, the Chinese were very subdued and refrained from making any public statements in support of Pakistan. This was in spite of India's ill-considered remarks on China as the cause of its going overtly nuclear in May 1998. Echoing Jiang Zemin, the Chinese Premier Zhu Rongji told his visiting Pakistani counterpart Nawaz Sharif in June 1999 that the Kashmir problem is "an issue left over from history concerning territory, ethnic nationalities and religion". Hence, the "rebuke with Chinese characteristics" that General Musharraf received is part of an emerging pattern. Chinese scholars and diplomats like Cheng Ruisheng writing in Chinese publications repeatedly invoke the "Deng" formula to stabilise Indo-Pak relations. This was the formula suggested by Deng Xiaoping to Atal Bihari Vajpayee in February 1979 and to Rajiv Gandhi in December 1988 to bring India and China closer together— set intractable issues aside, keep negotiating on them in good faith but *simultaneously* concentrate on trade and investment. The Chinese are at great pains to appear even-handed in the subcontinent. The unprecedented joint Sino-Indian naval exercises last month off Shanghai, for instance, were preceded by a similar Sino-Pak manoeuvre.

Why are the Chinese changing? Three main reasons.

First, they are being hurt considerably by Islamic terrorism in Xinjiang where Uighur separatists trained by the Taliban and by Pakistan-based outfits are very active. Xinjiang is important to China not just geographically as a gateway to Central Asia but also economically since it is rich in natural resources like oil and gas. The three evils as the Chinese call it - extremism, separatism and terrorism—are linked closely to Pakistan. Second, India itself looms large on China's radar screen. Already, the volume of Sino-Indian trade is over three and a half times the volume of Sino-Pak trade. But much more than growing trade and investment, the Chinese have newfound respect for India because of our success in software and high-tech. The Chinese would not like to sabotage a promising arena of economic cooperation, even if there is competition. Third, changing Sino-Pak ties symbolise a new Chinese approach to regional and global diplomacy, an approach that seeks to make up for its historical commitment to narco-militarist states like Pakistan, North Korea and Myanmar and to assuage "fears" of its galloping economic might.

China is not about to abandon Pakistan after having helped it build up a comprehensive strategic capability through the 1980s that included supply of heavy water, assistance for research reactors, plutonium reprocessing and uranium and transfer of missile production technology as well as supply of missiles themselves. Whatever China's protestations may be now, the evidence for its support to Pakistan in nuclear and missile technology is incontrovertible. This support has ended but strategic links remain. Just last month, an agreement was signed for a second 300 Mw nuclear reactor at Chashma southwest of Islamabad. Plans for building a deep-water port at Gwadar off the coast of Baluchistan are still active, although with the palpable US influence over Pakistan now, how the plans actually fructify remains to be seen.

China's foreign policy is in great flux. It is all part of a single-minded focus on economic development oriented to making China an economic superpower in every respect (except, perhaps per capita income) in the next two decades. China realises that peace in its region—East Asia, South Asia and Central Asia—is essential for sustaining such a unidirectional effort. It is all part of the new PRC syndrome—not the old People's Republic of China but a new Peaceful Rise of China. The Chinese establishment's mantra is *heping jueqi*—peaceful ascendancy. The new PRC will not be facilitated if it is seen to be extending support to forces ostracised by the international community. What the Chinese will do when they achieve overwhelming economic dominance is a separate issue. But for now, the substance is economics, the language is peace and stability, the style is constructive diplomacy. Economic clout and military muscle notwithstanding or perhaps precisely because of that, the Chinese want to be seen an good neighbours and sober citizens of the world. But there are two big question marks. Economic success is breeding aggressive nationalism that could easily run amok. And Taiwan's politics can still get the Chinese into apoplectic fits as recent events have demonstrated and this, in turn, fuels global fears of China.

Mekong versus Metookong

China appears more serious on
sub-regional cooperation than India

The historic city of Dali famous for its Three Pagodas
and located in the southwest Chinese province of Yunnan
recently hosted the ministerial meeting of the Greater
Mekong Subregion Economic Cooperation Programme.
Coordinated by the Asian Development Bank (ADB), this
programme involves China, Thailand, Vietnam, Laos,
Cambodia and Myanmar with Yunnan being the main
torchbearer on behalf of China. The programme was
launched in 1992 and over the past eleven years, around
$1 billion has been put on the ground in power and
transport projects. But it was only last November in Phnom
Penh that the six heads of state met for the first time to
give the programme a renewed political momentum and
chart a ten-year strategic framework for cooperation in
diverse areas like energy, health, education, environment,
transport, tourism and telecommunications. Coming
almost a year after this summit, the Dali meeting assumed
special importance. It reiterated the commitment of the
six countries to the three Cs-connectivity, competitiveness
and community—in the region.

In an apparent bid to counter the Chinese, India too
has made a foray into the Mekong Basin. In July 2000,

with much fanfare and recalling its ancient links to the region, India announced a Ganga-Mekong Swarnabhoomi Project involving India, Thailand, Vietnam, Laos, Cambodia and Myanmar leaving out China where, incidentally, the Mekong originates. The project was grand in scope envisaging cooperation in areas like road and rail infrastructure, tourism, IT and education. But unlike the Chinese-backed initiative in the Mekong Basin, the Indian-championed project is floundering. True, over the past year Mr. Atal Bihari Vajpayee has had successful visits to Cambodia, Laos and Thailand, apart from to China as well. The statement issued after the first ASEAN-India summit in Phnom Penh in November 2002 reaffirmed mutual interest in the Mekong-Ganga Project and also highlighted India's desire to participate in the Greater Mekong Programme. How these fine words and sentiments will translate into actual projects and investments by India remains to be seen. But Sanskritic chauvinism is the wrong way to go about winning friends. The website of the Indian Ministry of External Affairs makes the ludicrous claim that Mekong comes from Ma Ganga. And Mr. Jaswant Singh was forced to drop the word Swarnabhoomi when the Vientiane Declaration formally announcing the Mekong-Ganga initiative was adopted in November 2000.

China is championing another idea that is of great interest to India, particularly to our northeast and east whose economic future is tied as much to India as it is to East and Southeast Asia. In August 1999 academic scholars from four countries—China, India, Bangladesh and Myanmar - met in Kunming, the capital of Yunnan and adopted a document now referred to as the "Kunming Initiative". The provincial government of Yunnan has been the most enthusiastic votary of this initiative that contemplates cooperation in trade, tourism and transport. But the Indian government has been less than enthusiastic. The official establishment here sees the Kunming Initiative as a sinister ploy to increase Chinese influence in our troubled northeast. That China provided support to some militant groups in the northeast in the 1960s and 1970s is not in doubt. Whether it continues to do so is open to question. Whether it has larger designs on the northeast, barring perhaps on Tawang in Arunachal Pradesh (because of its historical and cultural ties with Tibet) is also debatable. After all, the package formula for solving the border dispute offered first by Zhou Enlai in 1960 and by Deng Xiaoping in 1979 did envisage the Chinese retaining the western sector and giving up its claims in the eastern sector.

Rich in biodiversity, Yunnan with a per capita income similar to that of India and a population of the size of Punjab and Haryana combined, is particularly fascinating. China has officially designated 56 ethnic groups as minority nationalities. Of these groups, the maximum number- 25 - are to be found in Yunnan alone, the ancestors of some of whom migrated to northeast India long ago. Yunnan was at the pivot of the southern Silk Route and the city of Lijiang played a key role in Sino-

Indian cultural history. Kunming is the home of the great
eunuch Muslim Admiral Zheng Hc who made seven epic
sea voyages from Taiwan to the Persian Gulf and Africa,
including repeated trips to Calicut. In more recent years,
it was to Kunming that Dr. Dwarkanath Kotnis,
immortalised in V. Shantaram's 1946 classic *Dr. Kotnis Ki
Amar Kahani,* first went in 1937, dispatched by Jawaharlal
Nehru as part of a medical relief mission. Dr. Kotnis is
still a hero in China but largely forgotten in his home
country. In 1992, the Chinese issued a stamp in his honour
and in January 2001, the visiting Chinese leader Li Peng
met his three sisters in Mumbai.

During 1942-44, the US Air Force regularly flew in
food, medical and other supplies from Kolkata to Kunming
over a treacherous Himalayan route that became
internationally known as "The Hump". This formed the
backdrop to James Hilton's haunting book *The Lost
Horizon* that gave the world Shangri La. Zhongdian is now
reckoned to be that haven of bliss and peace. In 1942-43
under the most harrowing of conditions, the US Army
led by the colourful Joe Stillwell constructed what has
come to be known as the Stilwell Road. This ran from
Ledo now in Arunachal Pradesh to Lashio in Myanmar
and then on to Kunming. The approximately 1700 - km -
long road (of which about 60 kms are in India, about 1000
kms in Myanmar and the rest in China) still exists but in
a state of extreme dilapidation.

Yunnan could well be India's gateway into China's
south and northwest which are already the focus of

massive development programmes. Although the WTO is increasing the powers of the central government in Beijing, China remains a country where the provinces have great economic autonomy, much more than what Indian states enjoy. A high-powered delegation from Chengdu, the capital of Sichuan and a major centre for scholarship on India, was in India to solicit investments in IT and other sectors and within days a team from Zhejiang province came to woo investors in the automotive industry particularly. Doing business with China really is doing business with its provinces, a reality that is yet to dawn fully in this country. Four years after the Kunming Initiative was first unveiled, it remains essentially an academic exercise on our side. Now, we have an excuse since Bangladesh appears to be reluctant to provide transit to Kolkata. If "Y2K" (Yunnan to Kolkata) is not possible immediately, we should go ahead with providing connectivity of the northeast to Myanmar and Yunnan hoping that Bangladesh would come around at some stage. As Beijing has "allowed" Yunnan to take the leadership role in the Kunming Initiative, why can't New Delhi give a similar role to West Bengal, Assam and other northeastern states? Similarly, in talks with Nepal on water management, why should UP and Bihar not take a more proactive role since their vital interests are involved? Subregional cooperation is not a recipe for the Balkanisation of India but it is a way of building new bridges, both physically and politically.

Section Two

The Great Trade Route to Chindia

Trade between China and India crossed the ten billion dollar mark at the end of 2004 and is poised to grow annually. The series of articles in this section looks at the huge potential for trade and other forms of economic exchange that exists between India and China, especially under the new WTO regime to which India and more recently, China are signatories. Jairam Ramesh points out how China is far ahead of India in several areas, especially because of its clear policies on labour laws, its openness to FDI and because China has not "remained a prisoner of shibboleths and sterile ideology". He highlights how this changed mindset has pushed China into advance gear while India continues to lag behind in comparison. The comparison here must also be based on the fact that India is a democracy where populist sentiments dominate government discourse. China, on the other hand, has the capacity to initiate policy reform in a unilateral fashion. This can be advantageous and disadvantageous, and the author discusses the pros and cons of both in this series of articles. He also points out how India's security concerns often impact foreign investment by China in India and suggests that Indian fears must not derail closer economic integration, especially since China fears no such threat from Indian business. As one of India's original supporters of economic reform, and an economic policy planner for the Government of India, the author is well placed to judge economic policies and strategies for growth in both countries objectively. He points out that China and India controlled world trade in the pre-colonial world, and today, are, once again set to take the lead in this field.

Jairam Ramesh sees closer economic cooperation between the two countries as the best way to build trust, friendship and a long and lasting peace between old friends, recent enemies, and now partners in the Asian century. Hence his very apt wordplay with Chindia.

Growing Ambivalence

India has embraced trade with China but does it fear Chinese investments?

Are we schizophrenic when it comes to full-fledged economic ties with China? The question must no longer be avoided. On the one hand, bilateral trade is galloping. The volume of two-way trade between India and China (excluding Hong Kong) in 2002 was close to $5 billion with Indian exports at around $2.3 billion and imports at around $2.7 billion. The January-March 2003 figures are even more impressive. Indian exports are valued at around $0.95 billion and imports at about $0.72 billion. Indian exports in January-March 2003 have zoomed 119% over January-March 2002, while imports have increased by 42.5%. Slightly less than 10% of India's total international trade is with "Greater China" comprising mainland China, Hong Kong and Taiwan. Thus, this trade is crucial for us, although it forms a miniscule proportion of international trade of that region—it accounts for considerably less than 0.5% of China's global trade, for example.

While trade has taken off, we seem to be prisoners of the old mindset when it comes to Chinese investments in India. Huawei Technologies, the Chinese telecom networking major already employs over 500 Indian software professionals in Bangalore but it has already caused concern in the Indian security establishment. We are approaching its expansion plans very warily. The Chinese consumer goods giant Haier, whose colourful CEO's life has recently been captured on celluloid, has been attempting to set up a production base in India but finds itself stymied for one reason or the other. Hutchison Port Holdings has just been debarred from participating in a major port development project with blue-chip Indian partners apparently on strategic objections by the Indian navy. Hutchison Telecom's pre-eminent position in the Indian mobile telephony market has is causing much discomfort to policy makers. There have been reports that Chinese companies are being discouraged in investing in hydel projects in "border" states like Himachal Pradesh, quite apart from also in road projects in states like Tamil Nadu. A Chinese company has evinced interest in the privatisation of the aluminium giant NALCO in Orissa causing some concern in official circles but that sale appears to have been aborted for the time being.

Indian ambivalence—more precisely, the ambivalence of the central government in its myriad forms—on Chinese investments in India is coming at a time when Indian companies are aggressively scouting for investment opportunities themselves in China. TCS is a leading candidate for bagging the prestigious contract for the computerisation of the Shanghai stock exchange. Ranbaxy was an early investor in China. TCS and NIIT already have a presence and Infosys has talked about an investment, although its plans unveiled with great fanfare in the presence of Zhu Rongji during his visit to Bangalore in January 2002 seem to have been delayed. Interestingly, Infosys blames the Chinese bureaucracy for the slow take-off but there may well be other contributory factors. Of late a slew of companies like Apollo Tyres, Sundram Fasteners and SRF have joined the investor community in China. Others like Dr. Reddy's Laboratories, JK Tyres and Aurobindo Pharma could soon enter. Tata Steel and Bharat Forge have notched major export successes and may well take the next step of a manufacturing presence in the Chinese market. It is true that we have not tested the Chinese and no Indian company has ventured forth to invest in Tibet or Xinjiang, two of the politically most sensitive regions of China. It is also true that we have been slow to develop commercial ties with Taiwan, something that might also test Chinese attitudes and responses. Even so, on the basis of present evidence it certainly appears that China is more relaxed about Indian investment presence in China than we appear to be on Chinese investment in India. Even on trade it must be said that while we are less inhibited, we have acquired the dubious distinction of being the single largest user of anti-dumping duties in the world—a truly remarkable phenomenon in a perverse kind of way given our laughably low share of global trade.

Of course, any bias against Chinese investments will be strenuously denied by officials in the capital. There is, of course, no clear policy directive or direction to this effect. They will point to the remarkable success of South

Korean companies like Hyundai and LG in India in the past few years as proof of our open door policy, especially to investors from East Asia. But there is no political paranoia in India vis-à-vis South Korea as there is in relation to China. Perceptions matter. The reality may well be different but in all such matters optics assume great importance. Whatever we say, the gnawing feeling in the community that is concerned about such matters is that India is still unable to break out of the shibboleths of the past. When business visas to China after proper documentation take four-five days to get here but when business visas to India there take two-three weeks, then there is bound to be a feeling that we are not on the same wavelength. The fact is we are not. Just consider the media presence in each other's countries. There is just one Indian journalist positioned in Beijing affiliated with the PTI while there are twelve Chinese journalists in New Delhi alone.

Against this background, the move by the Confederation of Indian Industry (CII) to open an office in Shanghai is a welcome step forward. China was a partner country in CII's India International Trade Fair earlier this year. In mid-October 2003, the first-ever Made in India show is being organised in Beijing with the support of the two governments. Hopefully, this show will travel to other provinces and growth centres in China. An India Club is also being launched in Shanghai located in the famous Shanghai Mart. This will undoubtedly be of great value to Indian business looking to export to, source from or invest in China. One of the objectives of the Club must be to address the fundamental asymmetry in the bilateral trade relationship and enhance India's importance in China's overall trade portfolio.

Over the past few days, there have been some reports emanating from South Block that India and China are close to a "deal" over Sikkim and some initiative in this regard may be announced during Mr. Vajpayee's visit to Beijing in late June. If the Chinese were to recognise that Sikkim is an unalienable part of India, the historic silk road that runs between Sikkim and Tibet through the Natu La pass could well be reopened by India with implications for tourism as well. But even without formal recognition, a border trade agreement will be in our long-term interest. While this must be pursued, it is important that Mr. Vajpayee's visit is used to allay Chinese fears that India is not favourably inclined to an increased Chinese investment presence here. If we do not send a positive signal forcefully and categorically, the expansion plans of Indian companies themselves in China will be under threat. You cannot open a green channel for trade and say that we will go slow on investment because we don't trust you fully. The two are inextricably linked.

Different Beds, Same Dreams

*Vajpayee tells Hu what Deng had said to
Rajiv fifteen years earlier*

In Beijing in December 1988, the octogenarian Deng Xiaoping told the 44 - year-old Rajiv Gandhi that " if there should be an 'Asian Age' in the next century, then it could be realised only after India and China became developed economies". When the soon-to-be octogenarian Atal Bihari Vajpayee met his 60 - year-old Chinese counterpart Hu Jintao in St. Petersburg, he remarked that "if the two countries were to cooperate this could even result in the 21st century turning into an 'Asian century'". Such hopes are, of course, not new. At least two other distinguished Indians in the 20th century—Rabindranath Tagore and Jawaharlal Nehru—had expressed similar sentiments more eloquently.

At the beginning of the 18th century, China and India certainly dominated the world and not just demographically as seen from the following table.

Distribution of World Income (%)
(based on purchasing power parity)

	1700	1820	1890	1952	1978	1995
China	23.1	32.4	13.2	5.2	5.0	10.9
India	22.6	15.7	11.0	3.8	3.4	4.6

Europe	23.3	26.6	40.3	29.7	27.9	23.8
USA	-	1.8	13.8	21.8	21.8	20.9
Japan	4.5	3.0	2.5	3.4	7.7	8.4
Russia	3.2	4.8	6.3	9.3	9.2	2.2

Source: Angus Maddison, *Chinese Economic Performance in the Long Run,* OECD Paris 1998 made available by Sanjaya Baru

In some ways, therefore, the 21st century should see the re-emergence not the emergence of China and India as economic powerhouses. Why and how these two countries simply lost out over the past three centuries is a subject of continuing debate and scholarly analysis. Recently, Kenneth Pomeranz's magisterial *The Great Divergence*, for example, has sparked a lively debate with his thesis that more than non-market and internal forces, its ecological environment and its colonies helped Europe surge ahead at the expense of both China and India.

Historical research apart, what of the future? Already, measured in the terms of international dollars or purchasing power parity (PPP), China is the second largest economy in the world, next to the USA. It is followed by Japan and India that crossed Germany three years ago. At present growth rates, India is poised to be the world's third largest economy by 2010 but the gap between it and China would still be substantial. But it is a moot point whether China and India will play the type of catalytic role in the regional and world economy that Japan, for instance, played in the 1970s and 1980s and whether they will emerge as engines of world growth alongside the USA and

Europe. On present reckoning, China is more likely to assume such a role than India over the next decade or two. Demographically, of course, India will almost certainly surpass China by the middle of this century and the two countries would then account for around 40% of world population. China is becoming the manufacturing fulcrum of the world with India becoming the pivot for knowledge-based industries, research and development, software and IT-enabled services. This does not mean that China will not make inroads into the world's services market or that India will not build up its own manufacturing capacity. What will actually materialise is a pattern of growth in the two countries that is both competitive and complementary at the same time.

China's politics and society is fundamentally different than in India. That is what makes a comparative evaluation of the performance of the two countries difficult. But this should not preclude a look at the comparative evolution. Till about the mid-1970s, India and China were almost on par. But since then, China's growth record has been spectacular while India's has been steady and robust. Rapid urban renewal makes the impact of growth in China far more dramatically visible than in India. One of the fascinating questions for students of contemporary economic history is this: why did China take-off in the mid-1970s after major agrarian reforms and why did West Bengal (and Kerala as well) *not* take-off even though they were then at a similar stage as China? This is, incidentally, a question first posed to this columnist some months back by Debu Bandyopadhyaya, one of the architects of West Bengal's highly acclaimed land reforms programme.

There is no mystery to why China has taken off in such a stunning manner. It has followed very pragmatic policies exemplified in Deng's famous aphorism—what does it matter if the cat is black or white as long as it catches mice? Unlike India, it has not had restrictive labour laws or policies like that of reservations for the small-scale sector. It has not strangulated its textile industry or crippled manufacturing by fiscal policy like we have. It has invested more. And it has exported (and imported more). The answer to Bandyopadhyaya's question is that unlike China, West Bengal has remained a prisoner of shibboleths and sterile ideologies. Mindsets may be changing slowly but setminds are wreaking havoc here.

It is now fashionable to decry Chinese statistics, although scholarly opinion is divided. Sure, GDP growth may well have been overstated by 1-2 percentage points. Foreign investment inflows too may be exaggerated—according to an IFC study done in 1997, roundtripping (that is, Chinese local investment going to Hong Kong and returning as "foreign" investment) reduces net FDI inflows from the reported annual average of around $40 billion to about $20 billion a year. But foreign trade figures are not suspect. All said and done, the Chinese economy is a "sweat" economy that grows more on the back of huge investments and less on the basis of productivity and efficiency.

Talk about "Asian age" or "Asian century" inevitably brings up the role of the diasporas. No question that the Chinese diaspora has made more constructive contributions than its Indian counterpart in both mobilising investment and boosting international trade. An estimated two-third to three-fourth of all foreign investment inflows into China emanates from Hong Kong, Taiwan and Singapore. If you believe the Chinese numbers anywhere between $25-30 billion of money pours into the Chinese economy from the overseas Chinese community which is about 50-55 million strong. But while the overseas Chinese have been large-scale investors, overseas Indians, because of their very nature, have been large-scale depositors and remitters. The stock of NRI deposits now amounts to about $28 billion. Those Indians who point to FDI roundtripping in China with great glee should know that such roundtripping could well be happening here as well in the case of NRI deposits. FDI investment through NRIs has been very small, amounting to no more than $3 billion over the past twelve years but since the mid-1990s another $3 billion of NRI money has come in for acquisition of shares. Remittances from workers overseas are more important with such inflows averaging about $7-8 billion annually.

Paradoxically, democratic India has been highly centralised while authoritarian China has been very decentralised. But transformations are taking place in both countries. India is becoming more polycentric while in response to the WTO accession China is becoming more of a centripetal system. Both countries are going through profound political, economic and social changes and each needs to understand the other better.

Currency Conundrums

Both China and India face tough
choices on exchange rates

The Chinese currency is under assault—both verbal and speculative. The US Treasury Secretary John Snow, the US Federal Reserve Bank Chairman Alan Greenspan and a couple of American Senators have called for a revaluation of the yuan/renminbi. The Governor of the European Central Bank Wim Duisenberg has joined the chorus as have senior ministers from Japan and South Korea. Influential investment banks have put out research reports suggesting that a revaluation is both needed and is imminent.

Unlike most currencies, the yuan is pegged at 8.28 to the US dollar, although it is allowed to vary within an extremely narrow band of 8.276-8.28. It has always been at the centre of debate. The roots of the East Asian financial crisis of 1997/98 have been traced back by some scholars to the hefty devaluation of the yuan by 50% in mid-1994. During the crisis and its aftermath, however, China earned plaudits for holding the peg and for dispelling fears that it would devalue yet again. But why, when it was praised for currency stability then, is it being criticised for currency stability now? Two major factors account for the view that the yuan is grossly undervalued: (i) the phenomenal rise in forex reserves and huge inflows of foreign capital; and (ii) persistently high growth rates of both GDP and of exports, especially to the US and to Europe.

China's foreign exchange reserves have increased from $217 billion in January 2002 to $340 billion in July 2003, with over half the increase taking place in the first half of the year alone. Andy Xie of Morgan Stanley and one of the sharpest China-analysts has taken the view that the rapid increase in forex reserves appears to be due to expectation shifts rather than change in fundamentals. China's forex reserves tend to rise in tandem with capital inflows rather than trade surpluses. He also argues that currency appreciation is not warranted because China's actual growth rate is still below the growth potential. What is happening is that FDI flows are very strong as global manufacturing capacity relocates to China driven partly by the absence of a currency risk. In addition, overseas Chinese are pouring money into acquiring properties at home. The perception that the yuan is undervalued and can only appreciate in the long-run is leading to a significant return flight of capital of both non-residents and residents. Will this prove to be a self-fulfilling prophecy?

China has a huge trade surplus with the USA (over $ 100 billion in 2002 and likely to be $120-130 billion in 2003). This has happened more because China has displaced Japan and other East Asian countries as a low-cost supplier and because it has embedded itself in the global supply chain of American companies. Further, China actually runs a trade deficit with other Asian countries and this includes India. The dollar has fallen steeply in global markets (25% against the euro and 10% against the yen in the past eighteen months) because of the very large American current account deficit. This deficit is now at around 5.5% of GDP and reflects the collapse of savings in the US both among households and corporates leading to a voracious appetite for borrowings from abroad. As the dollar has fallen in relation to the euro, China's competitiveness in European markets has also increased. As the dollar weakens, China gains.

What will the Chinese do? Fearing a revival of deflation from whose clutches it is just escaping and with a fragile financial sector that is in worse shape than India's, China may to do nothing, except widen the trading band or make it a "crawling" band. Movement to a floating exchange rate system is simply not on the cards. While senior officials have recognised the need for flexibility in the exchange rate, it is most unlikely that China would do any substantial upward adjustment in response to international pressure. But there are other options. Foreign exchange controls both the current and on the capital account could well be eased much along the lines of what has taken place in India. A disinvestment programme to sell something like $240 billion of government holdings in state-owned enterprises is on the anvil. As China's commitments to the WTO begin to unfold themselves more fully, import demand will also increase. This is already beginning to happen and China actually ran a small trade deficit in the first quarter of 2003. Regional monetary arrangements could also get a boost as East Asian countries think of alternatives to investing in low-yielding American treasury bonds. However, the more China grows, the greater will be the pressure for a revaluation.

India moved from a fixed exchange rate to a "managed float" between 1991 and 1993. The move has been a great success even though there are now pressures evident on the exchange rate front. The rupee has appreciated by almost 5% over the past year as dollars have flown in and forex reserves have zoomed. In the past twelve months alone, India's forex reserves have increased by $ 30 billion. The Reserve Bank of India has ascribed this to strong fundamentals—booming software earnings, increasing remittances from Indian workers overseas and strong foreign investment inflows reflecting global confidence in India. While all this is undeniable, the fact that Indian inflation-adjusted interest rates are 3-5 percentage points higher than in countries like the USA, has led to a surge in capital inflows. These inflows are best described as "arbitrage capital" as it may not be quite "hot" money as popularly understood and feared. Both NRIs (and their RI counterparts!!) and foreign institutional investors have brought in large sums to take advantage of attractive interest rates in India.

Such large inflows could have stoked inflation but the RBI has rightly prevented that from happening by "sterilising" the bulk of the inflows by the sale of government securities. Interest rates could have been dropped to moderate the inflows of arbitrage money. Indeed this has been the response in some East Asian countries where forex reserves have also shot up like in India. But because of the need to maintain high interest rates for provident fund and small savings, there are limits to how much interest rates will be allowed to fall. With inflation not increasing and interest rates not falling, something has to give and that something is the exchange rate. In the absence of a buoyant demand for dollars because of sluggish economic growth rates, the rupee has kept appreciating and if it continues to do so export growth could well be the casualty. In the short-run, a strengthening rupee may fuel pride but the exchange rate must be seen just as another price. There should be no stigma associated with a weakening currency. But currency management has to be part of a comprehensive strategy, embracing non-price factors as well, to boost global competitiveness. More than the exchange rate itself, China's stunning success in world markets is explained by these non-price factors (e.g. infrastructure, labour laws, small-scale reservation) and by a superior domestic taxation system in which a single VAT occupies a central place. In all these areas, we continue to be at a severe disadvantage.

FDI Revisionism

A Chinese-American academic is a
Sino-sceptic but an Indo-bull

Yasheng Huang, a Chinese-American and an
Associate Professor at the Harvard Business School is fast
becoming a favourite of Indians—both here and abroad.
This is because of his recent publications that assert that
China's achievements are exaggerated, while India's
advances have not received due recognition. He has co-
authored, along with his colleague Tarun Khanna, an
article "Can India Overtake China?" that appeared in the
July/August issue of the prestigious magazine *Foreign
Policy.* The dons argue that "China and India have pursued
radically different development strategies. India is not
outperforming China overall but it is doing better in
certain key areas. That success may enable to catch up
and perhaps even overtake China".

Now Professor Huang's more detailed book *Selling
China: Foreign Direct Investment During the Reform Era*
is also out. In this, Huang explains that the massive foreign
investment inflows into China are actually a sign of
structural weakness in the Chinese domestic economy and
do not in any way reflect a "boom". These inflows are, no
doubt, helping to make the economy more efficient. But
they have been a pervasive phenomena in China because

domestic private firms have been deliberately stifled and are simply uncompetitive to respond to new business opportunities. According to Huang, foreigners are investing more in China while domestic firms are investing less, although the distinction is blurred because of "round tripping"(the flight of resident capital and its return as foreign investment) via Hong Kong.

China has had a spectacular performance since 1978 when reforms were first introduced. In about a quarter of a century, GDP is estimated to have zoomed by an astronomical 8-9% compound annual average growth rate—translating to a doubling in less than ten years. But these numbers are being challenged. Thomas Rawski, a professor of economics at the University of Pittsburgh in the USA has concluded that Chinese GDP figures could be puffed up by at least 2-3 percentage points. Rawski's analysis, however, has been questioned by other eminent economists like Nicholas Lardy now at the Washington-based Institute of International Economics and author of a number of acclaimed works on the Chinese economy.

Then there is the American lawyer of Chinese descent, Gordon Chang who hit the headlines with his *The Coming Collapse of China.* Chang argued that the People's Republic has at most a decade before it crumbles. The trigger is the accession to the WTO that happened in December 2001 but there are other pressure points -a banking system that has all but failed, state-owned enterprises that are visibly dying, the Internet that is proliferating in spite of efforts to control it, a private sector that is strangulated, a society being wrecked by corruption and a state that is simply unable to accommodate the growing aspirations for freedom. Chang observes that China's economic success is built on very shaky and precarious political foundations and it is this that is causing growing unrest in that country.

It is not as if private Chinese companies do not exist. The top ten companies (groups) are Legend, Wanxiang, Hengdian, Chint, Delixi, Guanghui, Fosun, Xingaochao, China Orient and Tengen. However, the total turnover of these top ten is about half the turnover of the top ten Indian private companies. Huang talks of Indian private companies like Infosys and Wipro, Cipla, Ranbaxy and Biocon, and the Tata group as world-class firms owned and managed by Indians themselves. Since China has become the manufacturing platform for the world, a very large number of "Chinese" companies that are successful are actually affiliates or subsidiaries of companies from the USA, Japan, Germany and other countries. The Chinese corporate scene, however, is not entirely blank. Companies like Legend Computer, Haier, Kelon and Huawei - some of whom are coming to India as well— have emerged as global players. The Shanghai Stock Exchange is being engineered to be a global bourse in five years' time (if only the Indian government had been more proactive, TCS may well have won the contract for its computerisation that was awarded recently to American firms).

One of the reasons why China has attracted more

71

foreign investment than India is because in India there has been an influential business lobby against foreign investment, a lobby that has powerful political backers as well. This lobby is not as vociferous as it used to be but there are still a number of Indian companies who refuse to have anything to do with foreign investment. Sundram Fasteners, for example, has become a global supplier of radiator caps to General Motors and its success has not come out of any foreign investment inflow. Reliance is another example of such a company which has achieved global scale and standards without foreign investment. But there are other companies like Hindustan Lever that depend on foreign investment. Companies like Infosys and HDFC, of course, does not depend on FDI but more on FII—that is foreign institutional investors who invest for returns and not for management control.

Huang has certainly dealt a blow to the large tribe of Indo-critics and Indo-pessimists even though his sample of "successful" Indian companies is limited mainly to a couple of software and pharmaceutical firms. Certainly, India has had a long tradition of private enterprise and pre-1991 policies may have created the platform for entrepreneurial take-off. But there were many elements of the *ancien regime* that, ironically, helped Indian enterprise. The public sector, for example, has fostered entrepreneurship - the growth of Bangalore and Hyderabad has been heavily dependent on public investment in high-tech areas of defence, space and engineering.

Huang is right to focus on the domestic economy. Undoubtedly, entrepreneurial drive and dynamism in India is greater reflecting vastly more political and social freedoms here. But the business-like manner in which the Chinese are moving, using the WTO as a pretext to carry out sweeping reforms, is striking. This is in stark contrast to India where reforms of domestic taxation particularly have been stalled, as evidenced from what has happened to VAT. In addition, structural change in India has been skewed. Agriculture's share of GDP has fallen as it should. The share of services has risen disproportionately to over 50% of GDP at the cost of industry, especially manufacturing. At less than a fifth, India has the lowest share of manufacturing in GDP among all major countries. Manufacturing has staged a revival in recent years but there is still a very long way to go. Further, the share of agricultural employment has remained more or less unchanged because of rigid labour laws and small-scale reservations.

Huang raises an even more fundamental issue. How is that while India's growth is 80% that of China between 1997 and 1999 (actually, about two-thirds if a longer 1980-2000 period is taken), India achieved this on the basis of about half of China's savings and investment rate and less than 10% of China's foreign investment inflows. Does this mean that capital utilisation in India is more efficient than in China?

Foreign investment has made China the sixth largest trading nation in the world in a span of just over a decade.

It is galloping foreign trade fuelled by "foreign" investment that has transformed China in recent times. Huang's radical work cannot detract from that reality.

Their West, Our North

Regional disparities have a different meaning in China than in India

At about the same time that a regime change was being orchestrated in Lucknow in August 2003, the Chinese Prime Minister Wen Jiabao was announcing that a huge $85 billion has been spent over the past three years in China's much-talked about western region development programme. This is a massive investment campaign to deal with growing regional disparities in that country. China's populous regions are rich and dynamic. India's populous regions are poor and laggard, rich in identity politics but suffering from appalling governance. Although they are still poor and face formidable challenges, Rajasthan and Madhya Pradesh are definitely no longer prisoners of the BIMARU syndrome first identified by the noted demographer Ashish Bose almost two decades ago to describe the state of affairs in the Gang of Four—Bihar, Madhya Pradesh, Rajasthan and Uttar Pradesh. But Bihar and Uttar Pradesh—home presently to a quarter of India's population and between a third and two-fifths of its poor— have become "failed states". Regime changes are simply meaningless. What makes matters more serious is that for the next half a century at least the sheer demographic momentum will increase the share of the Hindi-belt states in India's population from some 40% now to perhaps about 60%.

China's western development programme was launched with great fanfare in 2000. It covers eleven administrative units: the five autonomous regions of Inner Mongolia, Tibet, Guangxi, Xinjiang and Ningxia, the five provinces of of Gansu, Guizhou, Shanxi, Sichuan and Yunnan and the Chongqing municipality. These all together account for something like 70% of the land area of the country but for less than a third of the population. These provinces are resource-rich and like the autonomous regions are home to China's numerous ethnic minorities. The focus in the programme is infrastructure and some of the more visible of the projects include the Qinghai-Lhasa railway and the west-east natural gas pipeline to exploit Xinjiang's rich hydrocarbon reserves.

According to an IMF study *Centripetal Forces in China's Economic Take-off* by Anuradha Dayal-Gulati and Aasim Husain published in May 2000 "after declining in the late 1970s and 1980s, the dispersion of provincial per capita incomes has increased steadily". They estimate that in 1978 real per capita income in the richest province was around nine times that of the poorest; by 1997 the multiple had risen to over eleven. When economic reforms were first launched by Deng Xiaoping, barring perhaps Shanghai the more advanced provinces of China were in its northeast, the region much like our own eastern region that received significant doses of public sector investment in coal and steel-based industries in the 1950s and the

1960s. But in two decades time, China's coastal provinces of Shandong, Guangdong, Fujian, Jiangsu, Zhejiang and Hainan along with the city-province of Shanghai surged ahead on the backs of foreign investment (largely from neighbouring Hong Kong and Taiwan), exports and the growth of township and village enterprises (TVEs) that ensured diffusion of prosperity within the regions. In India, when we talk about China, we automatically think of foreign investment and foreign trade. But the role of the TVEs has been equally crucial and they contrast with our own failed subsidy-based, protection-driven, scale-hampered, investment-starved rural industrialisation efforts carried out in a romantic Gandhian framework.

Regional disparities in India take on a different meaning. In China, even in the poor regions, real per capita incomes have increased by 5-7% compound per year over the past twenty years as compared to between 1-2% in states like Assam, Bihar, Orissa and UP. While regional disparities persisted during 1950-1990 in the heyday of the planning era and in some cases, paradoxically, even increased, the dispersion of real per capita incomes went up in the 1990s. The decade of the 90s brought them into sharper focus and in some cases accentuated them. But the normal perception that poor states became poorer and rich states became richer is not entirely true. This conclusion has to be nuanced somewhat. Punjab's compound annual growth rate decelerated from 5.7% in the 1980s to 4.9% in the 1990s. Haryana took an even steeper fall from 6.1% to 4.7%. Among the poorer states,

77

Madhya Pradesh improved its performance from 4.2% to
5.4%. In India, the real per capita income of the richest
state is about six times that of the poorest state. That is
because there is really no state in India that can equal
China's growth performance.

Even after accounting for exaggeration, real per capita
incomes in the coastal provinces of China have increased
by anywhere between 7-8% per year for 20 years which
means a quadrupling. In India, by contrast, real per capita
income in Gujarat and Maharashtra, our two most dynamic
states, have increased by 4-5% per year. Goa is perhaps
the only state to have Chinese-type growth numbers in
the 1990s but it hardly conveys the image of a booming
region. Relative rankings have been more stable in India
than in China although West Bengal's rank has come down
sharply much like China's northeast and Tamil Nadu,
Andhra Pradesh and Karnataka have all improved their
positions, Tamil Nadu most dramatically from number 11
three decades ago to number five now. But even here, you
don't get a feel of a boom—perhaps because urban renewal
does not take place as spectacularly in this country as in
China. The national bird of any booming economy, it is
said, is a crane. But construction technology in this country
is such that cranes are hardly visible in our cities!

China's western development programme is of more
than academic interest to India. Historically, this region
of China was traversed by the famous Silk Route that led
to enormous cultural, economic and technological cross-
fertilisation between the Indic and Sinic civilisations in

which, it is largely forgotten that Kashmir has played a crucial role. But more than history, the improvement of connectivity to provinces like Tibet, Yunnan and Sichuan will boost Sino-Indian trade. The Chinese have also been pushing the so-called "Kunming Initiative" named after the Yunnanese capital. This envisages investment and trade cooperation between Yunnan, Bangladesh, Myanmar and India's northeast. This initiative has meandered along for two-three years not the least because of lukewarm support from the Indian establishment suspicious of Chinese motives. What is unusual about this move is the keen interest being evinced by the province of Yunnan.

What will happen if sub-regional cooperation is fostered? India's northeast cannot develop except in a regional context. Even Bihar and UP need closer cooperation with Nepal on water management. Three years ago, India too came up with its grand Ganga-Mekong project to promote a broad range of cooperation in that region involving India, Myanmar, Thailand, Laos, Cambodia and Vietnam. How this will work leaving out China through which the Mekong runs and Bangladesh where the Ganges ends is a separate issue. But lofty announcements have to be backed by money allocations and expenditures on specific projects particularly in infrastructure like roads and highways. This has yet to materialise.

The Chinese central government has taken on a direct role in developing its backward regions. We had such an

79

approach in the 1950s but lost it along the way. It is time to rediscover that Nehruvian vision. Transferring more money to poorer states through the Finance Commission is no solution, nor is panchayati raj.

Blue Collar, White Collar

*China and India are raising fears in
America as job losses there mount*

As the WTO talks were collapsing in Cancun on September 14th, the US government announced the formation of a special task force to investigate Chinese trade policies that according to the Americans are unfair and impose a number of restrictions on foreign companies that prevent them from increasing their market presence in China. China also stands accused of refusing to let its pegged currency be revalued upward in relation to the dollar, of allowing software and music piracy to continue unchecked. The creation of an Unfair Trade Practices Team in the US Commerce Department comes in the wake of escalating alarm on the loss of some 2.7 million manufacturing jobs during the past three years since President George Bush took over, a decline last seen during President Herbert Hoover's tenure during the Great Depression over seven decades ago. American manufacturers have complained that low-cost imports from China are the main reason for such an unprecedented decimation. They have drawn support from politicians across the spectrum who are calling for higher duties on imports from China.

Economic recovery is very much on in the US and all

projections are that real GDP growth in the third and fourth quarters of 2003 will be somewhere around 5-6% on an annualised basis. Productivity growth is spectacular confounding most scholars. During 1995-2000, the period of the "great boom", productivity increased by about 2.5% per year. Since 2000, this has increased to 3.4% per year reflecting, in many ways, the long-hoped for payoffs from the huge investments made in IT in different sectors of the US economy. But by common consensus this is a "jobless" recovery. Productivity increases are taking place in an environment of growing job losses in industry that accounts for 40% of US GDP. Adding edge to the debate is the fact that the US Presidential campaign has already commenced and Democratic candidates are aggressively targeting President Bush on the gloomy employment situation.

Actually, India is also beginning to draw flak, perhaps not as much as China as yet but it is under attack nevertheless. The growing American fear is that as "blue collar" manufacturing jobs are being lost to China, "white collar" service jobs are being lost to India. The loss of service jobs has not been as dramatic as in manufacturing. Some estimates, like that made by Forrester, a leading US IT consultancy firm, are that about 400,000 jobs may have been offshored already. Over the next decade, 200,000 service jobs may be outsourced annually in the IT and IT-enabled services area. India could account for anywhere between a third and a half of these jobs. State governments in the US like that of New Jersey, Maryland, Connecticut,

Washington and Missouri have sponsored or are considering legislation to prohibit or restrict the state government concerned from contracting with companies that outsource to countries like India. The federal government has been silent. But while announcing the special task force in Detroit, the US Commerce Secretary Donald Evans said: "American manufacturers can compete against any country's white collars and blue collars, but we will not submit to competing against any country's choke collars".

So, while the immediate focus of the task force is China, the prospects of India also coming under the scanner for its trade, investment and market access restrictions cannot be ruled out. In this context, a recent research study by the Washington-based McKinsey Global Institute entitled *Offshoring: Is It a Win-Win Game?* is very timely and comes as a shot in the arm for those who have to combat growing protectionism in the USA. This estimates that offshoring creates net additional value for the US economy that did not exist before, a full 12-14 cents on every dollar offshored. The study shows that of the full $1.45-1.47 of value created globally from offshoring $1 of US labour cost, the US alone captures $1.12-$1.14, while receiving countries like India capture, on an average, just 33 cents. The American media is increasingly highlighting the shift of skilled service jobs to India. Most of these reports are alarmist, although recently the *Los Angeles Times* carried an article on how Oracle's hiring of more engineers in Bangalore is good for

Oracle in the US. It also drew attention to the creation of new businesses by Indian-American entrepreneurs in the USA that create new jobs in both America and in India. But such balanced pieces are very infrequent.

At the recent meeting of the WTO at Cancun, China was assertive but not argumentative. It kept a relatively low-profile. It was certainly part of the G-22, the group of 22 developing countries led by Brazil that included India and which confronted the US and Europe on the issue of farm subsidies and other issues. But its style was relatively less confrontationist than that of other G-22 members. It ran with the G-22 hare and hunted with the American hound. The terms of WTO accession agreed to by China are sweeping. China has undertaken to fulfil a very large number of market-opening obligations by 2006. It definitely is in no mood of taking on any additional commitments and to that extent it is with the G-22. At the same time it is conscious of the deepening political backlash against the enormous trade surplus that it enjoys with the US. This surplus could well be in the region of $130-150 billion in 2003 and a full one-fifth of the US trade deficit is on the China account alone. The US market is key to China's prosperity. For this reason, at key moments, China went along with the US at Cancun and while most G-21 ministers decried the stance of the rich countries, the Chinese Commerce Minister Lu Fuyuan donned a statesmanlike-mantle and declared that a stalemate was in no one's interest. Unlike India, China wants genuine liberalisation in global farm trade. India wants advanced countries to cut import tariffs and subsidies while retaining the right to have high tariffs and subsidies for itself. China wants free trade in agriculture and is prepared to cut subsidies at home knowing that it cannot sustain them for ever. In addition, its whole objective is to get more and more people out of agriculture, something that government policy actively discourages in India.

What should India do, apart from playing it low-key on job relocation and apart from lobbying with the US Congress? Clearly, India's merchandise imports from the US, that in 2002 amounted to just about $4 billion (as compared to India's merchandise exports of almost $12 billion) must increase both in the civilian and defence sectors. US service exports to India in 2002 amounted to $3 billion and this too could increase. More than that, Indian companies must begin to acquire companies in the US particularly in the manufacturing industry like auto components, engineering and textiles. Chapter 11 companies (that is, companies that have declared bankruptcy but still have great potential for revival) are a pool from which such acquisitions can be made. This could help mitigate the negative impact of growing outsourcing. Keeping aside what happened at Cancun, India has to keep the US engaged intensively on trade and commercial issues.

Crude Realities

Both China and India are and will
continue to be very major oil importers

A little more than ten years ago, an event of profound significance took place in China. This has already had great political and economic impacts, impacts that will be felt even more increasingly across the world. China became an oil importer in 1993. It was an oil importer for much of the 1950s till the discovery of the onshore Daqing mega oilfield in the northeast region in the late 1950s/early 1960s. This catapulted China into the major league of oil producers. For a while in the 1970s and 1980s, it even became a modest exporter. But the story is now dramatically different. In 2002, while China was the world's sixth largest oil producer, producing about 3.4 million barrels per day (mbd), it was also the world's fifth largest importer, buying close to 1.9 mbd.

Oil consumption is galloping and this year China is poised to overtake Japan as the world's second largest oil consumer. Projections are that by the end of this decade, China could be importing around half of its oil needs and perhaps as much as three-fourths by 2020. Today, a little less than 60% of imports are from the Middle East (mainly Oman, Yemen, Saudi Arabia and Iran) but China is looking to Russia, Central Asia, East Asia and Africa, apart from investing heavily in developing the hydrocarbon reserves in its own Xinjiang province where Muslim separatist movements have been active. However, Xinjiang is geologically complex and international oil companies have been lukewarm. Chinese claims in offshore South China Sea have met with resistance from Malaysia, Philippines, Vietnam, Taiwan and Indonesia and from Taiwan in the offshore East China Sea. While China would like to diversify, for the remainder of this decade, dependence on the Middle East will grow. With increasing US strategic domination in this crucial region and with its control over the sea-lanes from the Persian Gulf to the South China Sea, the Chinese are certainly worried. What has added to their discomfort is the growing bonhomie between the US and Indian navies reflected, for instance, in the Indian escort of American ships through the Straits of Malacca.

For long, the Russians have feared a massive Chinese demographic invasion in Siberia and their Far East. This fear has become a reality as reported by Vladimir Radyuhin, the Moscow correspondent of *The Hindu.* According to the Russian Census of 2002 to be released shortly, the Chinese have become the fourth largest ethnic group in Russia after the Russians, Tatars and the Ukrainians. Over 3 million Chinese have settled down in Siberia and the Far East since the late 1980s. No doubt the opening of the 4300-km border to bilateral trade is leading to the "Sinification" of places like Vladivostok, Khabarovsk, Irkutsk and the Sakhalin Island. But there is a larger strategic picture in the minds of the Chinese who are well aware of this Russian region's enormous oil and gas potential. China has been negotiating for building a 2300-km oil pipeline from the East Siberian town of Angarsk to Daqing at an estimated cost of about $2.5 billion. The Russians, keen on getting foreign investment into this remote region, are also looking at an alternative involving a pipeline to Nakhodka on the Pacific Coast. This alternative would deliver oil to Japan and South Korea as well. The Chinese are most unhappy at this development.

China is looking at other regions as well. The flagship China National Petroleum Corporation, whose subsidiary Petrochina is listed on the New York Stock Exchange, has pledged close to $ 8 billion to acquire potentially lucrative oil concessions in Kazakhstan, Venezuela, Sudan and Iraq. Of these, the Kazakhstan ventures are the most significant and the Chinese have gigantic, almost grandiose plans involving long pipelines. They are planning a 3000-km pipeline linking the Kazakh oilfields to Xinjiang as also a 1000-km pipeline linking Kazakhstan to Iran. This latter pipeline is part of a strategy to integrate the Middle East into China's Central Asian operations. The economic dimension that it is seeking to impart to the six-nation Shanghai Cooperation Organisation that was originally conceived of as a security and anti-terrorist grouping shows how China is viewing Central Asia where the dynamics have been changed following the establishment of the American military presence in Uzbekistan and Afghanistan in the last three years. In addition, the

Chinese National Offshore Oil Corporation has acquired hydrocarbon concessions in Indonesia, the Gulf of Mexico, Iran and Myanmar.

Some years ago, India imported 1.4 mbd out of a total oil consumption of about 2.1 mbd. Two-thirds of oil production in India is offshore as compared to less than 10% in China. This has given India enormous technological capability but it is not a major producer of oil. It ranks ninth among all importers of oil and by the end of the decade could well inch up to fifth or sixth place even assuming that new domestic sources are developed. Between three-fifths to three-fourths of India's oil needs will continue to be met through imports. Overseas acquisitions of oil fields is now an integral part of India's strategy as well and close to $3 billion has been committed so far. Of this, almost half is in the offshore Sakhalin Island in Russia's Far East that could start yielding considerable oil in the next three-four years. Along with Exxon that has a 30% stake, ONGC Videsh has a 20% share in this project which is the single largest foreign investment in the region. The other big Indian overseas investment is in the onshore Greater Nile Project in Sudan where, ONGC Videsh holds a 25% stake along with, interestingly, China National Petroleum Corporation that holds 40% and Malaysia's Petronas which has a 30% stake. Concessions in Iran's Farsi offshore fields in the Persian Gulf and in onshore Libya are under finalisation. In November 2000, Iraq and India signed an agreement that gave India a promising oilfield in western Iraq to develop. The fate of this agreement is now uncertain. In addition, Reliance already has an oil concession in Yemen. The Sudan project, from which oil in sizeable quantities, has already started flowing points to the potential for Sino-Indian cooperation in other places as well.

Natural gas will be an increasingly important energy source for both China and India even though in the transport sector, there is unlikely to be a commercially viable alternative to oil for the next decade at least. Both countries could well become part of regional natural gas networks. China's investments in Russia, Central Asia and East Asia encompass gas as well, while India has a producing gas field in Vietnam and is exploring for gas in Myanmar. But India's participation in cross-country networks is politically contentious. In the east, Bangladesh is unwilling, while in the west and in the north India is reluctant because any onshore pipeline from say, Iran and Turkmenistan will have to go through Pakistan and Afghanistan respectively.

Oil will fuel global diplomacy of both China and India. So far China has been more aggressive but India has not lagged that much behind. No doubt, it is an area of vulnerability for both countries but it also presents numerous opportunities for establishing and projecting their international presence.

Steel's Irony

*Indian steel exports to China zoom and
the Chinese are showing concern*

Question: Which is the world's largest consumer of steel?

Answer: China.

Question: Which is the world's largest producer of steel?

Answer: China.

Nothing surprising so far. But here is a new one.

Question: Which country became the world's largest importer of steel in 2002?

Answer: China.

This has happened because steel imports by the USA have dropped following protectionist measures adopted by that country. But with Olympics 2008 in Beijing, the trend should continue.

But here is something totally unexpected.

Question: Which country has the highest rate of increase in market share of Chinese steel imports in 2003?

Answer: You would never have guessed - India

In 2003, China's steel consumption is estimated at

almost 240 million tonnes which is almost a whopping eight times India's pathetically low consumption. This year, China's steel imports are expected to be around 32-34 million tonnes which will be more than all the steel we will consume. This is phenomenal growth by any standards. In 1990, steel consumption was just at about 50 million tonnes. This doubled by 1993. The years 1993-97 showed minimal growth. But during 1997-2002 yet another doubling took place.

The phenomenal difference in steel use between China and India does not reflect Indian efficiency or some new economic growth trajectory invented by us. It reflects the huge gap in infrastructure, in manufacturing, in industry, in construction and in investment spending. In many ways, the difference in steel consumption sums up the economic story of the two countries—what is particularly ironic is that an NRI group—owned by L.N Mittal—is now the world's second largest steel producer.

In the past fifteen months, India had gained significantly from the growth in the Chinese steel market so much so that presently about half of India's exports of steel go to China. Steel exports have caused the trade balance to swing in India's favour for the first time in 2003 so far. Going by Indian figures, India exported just 20,000 tonnes of steel in 2000 to China. This trebled to 64,000 tonnes in 2001. But in 2002, there was a massive jump to about 262,000 tonnes and even further to 709,000 tonnes during January-July 2003. The big five accounting for around three-fifths of all steel exports to China are SAIL, Ispat, Tata Steel, Jindals and Essar.

The figures being used by the Chinese are different and show even greater penetration of Indian steel in Chinese markets. For the period January-September 2003, the China Iron and Steel Association reports Indian exports of 1.58 million tonnes. For 2002, the Chinese figure is 480,000 tonnes, as compared to the Indian figure of 262,000 tonnes. Indian exports have been mainly in hot rolled coils/sheets, cold rolled coils/sheets, galvanised products and even stainless steel. The Indian companies have been so successful that the Chinese have begun to worry. They have asked the Indian companies to slow down their exports. The Indian companies, not wanting to antagonise a newly found market, have been defensive saying that as the Indian steel market picks up, exports to China would automatically get moderated. Price and "dumping" of steel is not the issue—if anything, China benefits on this score since India is now among the lowest cost producers of steel and Indian prices can be used by China as a benchmark.

What is irking the Chinese seems to be market shares. In 2002, India accounted for just about 2% of China's steel imports. But in 2003 so far, India's market share has jumped to 6-7%, close to that of Russia but well below that of Japan, Taiwan and South Korea. This has caused Chinese discomfort. The Chinese maintain that they are entitled to take protective measures under the WTO when imports of steel from a particular country cross 3% of all steel imports. They are technically right. India says anti-dumping duties can be imposed only after determining "material injury" in relation to imports as a proportion of consumption or production. This position is also right. Upto November 2002, China imposed "safeguards" duties of between 10-23% on selected categories of steel imports from countries like Japan, South Korea and Germany. India was spared at that time on the grounds that it was a "developing country". Indian companies gained. But they have become the victims of their own success.

Why is China expressing concern regarding steel imports from India? Perhaps, it finds it galling that of all countries India has done so well in its steel market. It is not that India is a threat. New capacity is coming on stream in China itself and while old capacity will be moth-balled, the notion that the Indian steel industry is a significant competitive threat to China is laughable. The roots of China's changing stance on galloping steel imports from India lie beyond steel. It lies in the Chinese belief, not entirely unfounded, that India continues to have reservations about Chinese investments in our country, whether it is power, consumer goods, telecom, software, ports and mining. Clearly, the momentum and goodwill generated by high-level political visits has not had any impact on our bureaucracy and security establishment. The Chinese are also unhappy that China attracts the maximum number of anti-dumping investigations by India - in the last five years, China accounts for about a fifth of all Indian anti-dumping duty cases. We look at China in sectoral compartments—steel, chemicals, software, etc. On the other hand, the Chinese have a holistic approach.

China's steel industry offers new avenues for investment cooperation with India. China requires iron ore desperately—high-grade reserves are scarce. Roughly one-third of iron ore requirements are presently imported largely from Australia, Brazil, India and South Africa, with India accounting for about a seventh of imports. Imports are bound to increase and some estimates are that by the end of the decade the proportion of imports could well exceed 50%. Clearly, India offers a number of advantages as a source of iron ore. One option would be to entice China into long-term contracts of the type we have with Japan and South Korea with the prospect of China investing in mine development and exploitation, apart from ports as well. Chinese steel companies like Baosteel have already made major joint venture investments to acquire and develop iron ore mines in Australia and Brazil.

But a better option was suggested very recently by B. Muthuraman, the dynamic Managing Director of Tata Steel and one of India's most outstanding techno-managers. In a round table discussion between Indian steel exporters and the China Iron and Steel Association organised by the Confederation of Indian Industry (CII) on October 17th at Beijing, he advocated a joint venture to produce semi-finished steel in India and finished steel in China. This way the legitimate concern that we should export value-added and not just natural resources gets addressed. It also ensures China's security of iron ore

97

supply. Since 2001 a number of steel joint ventures between Chinese companies on the one hand, and Japanese, German and South Korean companies on the other, have been announced and launched. The Muthuraman proposal is a "win-win" proposition for both countries and should be actively pursued by our government.

Not so Happy a Birthday

Today is the second anniversary of
China's accession to the WTO

Today marks the second anniversary of China's accession to the WTO when it became the 143rd member of that world body. The negotiations for the accession took fifteen long years and were marked by many twists and turns. Finally, China agreed to the terms of entry that were very onerous, much more onerous than India would have ever accepted. For instance, on farm subsidies, China has agreed to a maximum level of 8.5% of the value of production, as compared to 5% for the developed countries and 10% for developing countries like India. It has agreed to an average bound (that is, maximum) tariff level of 15% for agricultural products, as compared to India's 115%. Even after the developed countries abolish all textile import quotas on January 1, 2005, China will not be free of restrictions till December 31, 2008. For twelve years, WTO members will have access to a safeguard mechanism to protect themselves from Chinese imports. Foreign companies will have freedom for domestic retailing over a three-year period. Market opening in services - like telecom, banking, insurance and law - is more comprehensive than that being offered by India. It already offers product patents in pharmaceuticals unlike India which will do so from January 1, 2005. China has also agreed to a ten-year review of implementation of its accession protocol by the WTO.

The implementation of China's accession protocol is watched minutely across the world but most intensively in the US. The US Congress, the US Trade Representative, the US-China Business Council and other trade bodies all prepare annual review reports. The report last year gave China high marks but this year's progress report is more critical, pinpointing many areas where China is sliding back from meeting its WTO obligations in letter and spirit. The influential US-China Business Council gives China a score of just a little over five on ten for implementation in year two and says that most of the problems arise in Beijing and not at the local level as originally feared.

This year, Sino-US trade economic ties have come under pressure given that the bilateral trade deficit in favour of China has touched about $ 120 billion. The US has slapped extra duties on the import of certain textile imports from China, like bras and knitted fabrics and on colour TVs. There has been a clamour in the US Congress for an across-the-board hike in import duties on all US imports from China on the grounds that the Chinese renminbi that is pegged to the US dollar is substantially undervalued. The US government has expressed concern at the flight of US manufacturing jobs to China, no matter that American companies themselves are involved in this migration. For their part, the Chinese have postponed buying American commodities such as soybean, wheat and cotton.

100

In general, on tariffs, China scores high in implementation. Actually, China's tariff reforms predate entry into WTO. Even before WTO accession, for instance, China's average import tariff rate had fallen to around 15% in 2001, a year in which the corresponding figure for India was more than double the Chinese level. By 2005, average import duty rates in China are expected to settle at around 10%, which would be around one-third the Indian average. Transparency in laws and regulations remains the most serious problem. In spite of legislation, patent infringement, copyright piracy and trademark counterfeiting is rampant particularly in software, pharmaceuticals and consumer goods. The grant of trading and distribution rights to foreign companies supposed to have been in place by December 31, 2004 is way behind schedule. Adequate tariff-rate quotas (TRQs) in sectors like agriculture and automobiles (which allow a certain quantity of imports at lower duties) are not in place.

Traditionally, China has been at the receiving end of anti-dumping investigations by its trading partners. But in the first half of 2003, it became the third largest user of the anti-dumping mechanism, next to the USA and India. Since January 1, 1995 when the WTO came into being India has been the largest user of anti-dumping duties. India should be in the forefront to have the WTO get rid of anti-dumping, leaving the safeguard duty as a protective mechanism. But if we are such an enthusiastic user of anti-dumping—15% of all world cases during January 1995-June 2003 - especially ludicrous given our paltry less than

1% share of world imports, then we can hardly speak from a position of any legitimacy. The same principle applies for agricultural trade liberalisation. India's position is weakened considerably by her ridiculously high binding rates and by the fact that average applied agricultural tariffs (unweighted) have actually been increasing in recent years and are around 45-50%.

A direct consequence of China's accession to the WTO is its even closer integration with Taiwan which also became a WTO member soon after China. The WTO calls it "Chinese Taipei". Hong Kong and Macau are also separate members. Taiwan is the second or third largest investor on the Chinese mainland, accounting for about a fifth of all foreign direct investment flowing into China over the past two decades. Trade links are also very close. Before WTO entry, Taiwan was China's fifth largest trading partner after Japan, USA, Hong Kong and South Korea. In 2002, it moved up to fourth place and 2003 has seen growth continue robustly with a massive trade surplus in favour of Taiwan. Taiwan is now the second most important source of imports for China after Japan. Increasingly, components and semi-finished goods are moving from Taiwan to the mainland for processing and ultimate exports, as China's exports, to overseas markets, particularly the United States. In the IT industry especially significant relocation is taking place from Taiwan to China across all segments including semiconductor manufacturing. This gives China's IT hardware industry an added competitive edge which India will have to reckon with. With the growing use of embedded software, the conventional distinction between software and hardware in the IT industry is breaking down. If India were to look at embedded software as an area of global leadership, then perhaps its huge disadvantage in conventional hardware need not be crippling.

Aware that 2004 is a US Presidential election year that will see competitive China-bashing, China has stepped up its economic diplomacy. Its Premier Wen Jiabao is in America this week. Other channels are also at work. India could learn from China in this regard. One unfortunate fallout from the recent Cancun Summit of the WTO is that the US thinks India was not constructive in ensuring that a deal was clinched. Indian perceptions are different but the reality is that Bob Zoellick, the US Trade Representative is offended with our stance. India was the first country he visited after taking over three years ago and even earlier as President Bush's advisor he had written in *Foreign Affairs* in January/February 2000 that the US must work towards a special trade pact with India. It is not in our interest to have such an influential "friend of India" frustrated with us. What is needed apart from official talks, is quiet back-channel diplomacy also holding out the promise of procurement from the USA, which the Chinese excel at, to rebuild a strained Indo-US trade relationship.

Section Three

And Some Other Things

In this section Jairam Ramesh looks at issues that are not directly related to Sino-Indian relations. Instead, they deal with issues within China. His article on Islam and the Islamic minority known as Hui, in China will be an eye-opener for his Indian readers. Jairam points out the important role that Islam has played in Chinese history. Next he looks at the issue of Democracy in China. This issue became especially importance after the famous Tiananmen incident of 1989 when Chinese students were gathered in the heart of Beijing demanding democratic freedom. The movement collapsed and many students lost their lives in the bargain. However, today, while the government has made it clear that the Communist Party of China remains in control of the political administrative system, experiments with direct elections for the post of mayors in townships and in cities have been successfully carried out. The author skilfully analyses the future of this process in China. His article on HIV AIDS deals with a problem that both India and China face today. The author discusses the necessity of both countries combating this problem on a war footing, and here he gives more credit to China's war on AIDS.

His article on China's economic data and the need to critically examine its sources is also timely. He points out how and what we make of China's growth figures and how we see China's future as an economic power house.

This section of articles can be read as concluding pieces that indicate the extent and interest of the author in his subject and also once again showcase his commitment to the project of CHINDIA.

Mao Meets Mohammed

Few associate Islam with China
but there is a strong connection

September 11, 2001 revived global interest in Islam but because 90-91 per cent of its population belongs to the Han ethnic group, we do not read much about China in this context. China has been facing "Muslim" unrest in the strategically important, resource-rich north-west province of Xinjiang for a long time. Beijing witnessed major protests in May 1989 against Salman Rushdie's book *Satanic Verses* and the Tiananmen Square pro-democracy revolt of June 1989 was spearheaded by a Uyghur. China's long and durable relationship with Pakistan, seen by us solely in anti-Indian terms, actually has a distinct Muslim and West Asia perspective as well, as pointed out by John W. Garver in his very recent *Protracted Contest* in which he also points out that China's diplomatic and deterrent support for Pakistan has weakened just as its military assistance has not diminished.

There are differing estimates on the size of China's Muslim community since the Chinese census canvasses ethnicity and not religion. Official figures are about 20 million, which is slightly less than 2 per cent of the total population. The Indian scholar Rafiq Zakaria in his *The Struggle for Islam* places the proportion at at 10 per cent.

Dru Gladney of the University of Hawaii, an acknowledged authority, in his *Muslim Chinese* gives a range of 2-4 per cent.

Around half of the Muslim Chinese belong to the Hui nationality who have their own autonomous region of Ningxia. The Uyghurs are the second-most populous Muslim nationality and dominate Xinjiang. Han migration promoted by Beijing has radically altered the demographic mix in Xinjiang as it has in Xizang (Tibet). Other provinces with a significant Muslim population include Gansu, Qinghai, Yunnan, Guizhou and Beijing itself. Guizhou is China's poorest province, followed by Xizang, Gansu, Shaanxi, Ningxia, Sichuan, Yunnan, Qinghai, Chongqing and Xinjiang. The gap between these provinces and Shanghai and Guangdong has increased in the past two decades. That is why the focus of China's Tenth Five Year Plan (2001-05) is the massive development of its western region that covers these provinces. India's own growth plans for its eastern and northeastern regions can be linked to China's "remake the west" campaign.

Muslims have played a crucial role in Chinese history. The most colourful of them is perhaps the eunuch admiral Zheng He, the subject of Louise Levathes' fascinating book *When China Ruled the Seas: Between 1405 and 1433,* Zheng He's fleet made seven epic voyages reaching all the way up to the east African coast. It was a stunning achievement. The first two expeditions brought Zheng He to Calicut. The Chinese wanted cardamom, cinnamon, ginger, turmeric and pepper, while they offered silk, porcelain and lacquerware. Calicut is described in glowing terms in the chronicles of the admiral's colleague, another Muslim, Ma Huan. Zheng He was to die in Calicut itself in 1433 but was buried in Nanjing. Incidentally, the Kerala-China link has an even more ancient history—according to legend Damo, among the most revered Buddhist figures in China, was originally a Namboodiri. In contemporary times as well, distinguished Keralites have moulded our China policy—K.M. Panikkar, Krishna Menon and the K.P.S. Menon clan, with the grandfather serving as our envoy in Beijing during 1947-48, the son during 1985-87 and the grandson now in his third stint in Beijing as ambassador.

In June 2001, presidents of six countries—China, Russia, Turkmenistan, Uzbekistan, Kazakhstan and Kyrgyzstan—formally launched the Shanghai Cooperation Organisation (SCO). This is basically a Chinese initiative in order to build bilateral relations, promote regional cooperation to China's advantage specially with reference to Central Asian hydrocarbon resources and counter America's influence in world and regional affairs. This assumes special importance given that China's net oil imports now account for about a sixth of consumption and are growing. The SCO's main objective is to fight a war against the three evils of international terrorism, religious extremism and ethnic separatism.

Following September 11, which has led to an increased US military presence in Pakistan, Afghanistan, Uzbekistan and Kyrgyzstan, and with the growing bonhomie between America and Russia, the SCO faces an identity crisis. China's designs on resource-rich Siberia are a flashpoint in its relationship with Russia and Japan is very much part of this equation. There are also question marks over China's relationship with Pakistan. What will happen, for instance, to the Chinese project to develop the strategic Gwadar port on the Baluchistan coast near the Iranian border? The SCO is obviously of interest to India but we must not be ensnared into any arrangement that has anti-American overtones, just as we have to resist American efforts to build us up as a bulwark or counter-weight to China as well as the efforts of our own Sino-phobes to match China's military buildup.

Confucian Oxymoron

Is Chinese democracy a contradiction in terms?

First, it was the SARS epidemic that forced a whole new culture of transparency on Hu Jintao and his colleagues. Then it was Mr. Vajpayee's visit to Beijing that showcased India's plurality. Now it is massive public protests in Hong Kong. The "democracy deficit" in China has once again come under sharp focus, leading to renewed questions as to how long a vibrant market economy and an authoritarian, if not totalitarian polity can coexist.

China is neither an electoral nor a liberal democracy as India is. There have been public dissent and protest movements that have erupted every once in a while but they have all been brutally suppressed as was done to students at Beijing's historic Tiananmen Square in May 1989 and to the Buddhist-influenced *Falungong* in April 1999. For a very brief while in 1998 it looked as if a competitor to the Chinese Communist Party(CCP) in the form of the Chinese Democratic Party (CDP) would emerge but the CDP was soon banned. The CDP, however, is very active in the USA and elsewhere. But paradoxes— mostly unappreciated in this country particularly - abound. The Chinese Communist Party has been able to challenge its icons in a manner that no Indian political party has done or can do. Historically, Chinese provinces have enjoyed greater economic and administrative powers than the states in India. The CCP has been as faction-ridden as some major Indian political parties. Policy making in China has been a pluralistic, often acrimonious process but with definite finality, unlike in India.

In the past decade, China has seen what the noted American political scientist Suzanne Ogden has called the "inklings of democracy". While rule of law is a distant dream, rule by law—as crafted, interpreted and adjudicated by the CCP—is a reality. The man responsible for this was Peng Zhen who had been Mayor of Beijing in the 1950s and 1960s. If Mao made China strong, if Zhou made it internationally acceptable and if Deng made it rich, posterity will record that Peng laid the foundations of "democracy with Chinese characteristics". And there could not have been a more unlikely candidate for this honour. A die-hard Marxist, a victim of the Cultural Revolution for supporting critics of Mao, he rebounded in the late 1970s and ended his long political career as head of the National Peoples Congress durng 1983-88.

Between 1982-87, there was a heated debate in China on what the ongoing decollectivisation and the newly-introduced "household responsibility" system meant for rural self-governance. This system freed peasants from most production and distribution controls. Peng took the position that village democracy was essential for consolidating on the spectacular gains from farm liberalisation. Opposition was intense. Finally, a law was passed in November 1987 to introduce village-level

114

elections. Reflecting the widespread ambivalence it was called a provisional law. This law was regularised in 1998. Other than Peng (and Deng himself) only the Ministry of Civil Affairs under Cui Naifu showed enthusiasm for this revolutionary step. Finally, the support of influential leaders like Bo Yibo tilted the balance in favour of the political reformers. The motivations for taking such a step are now being unravelled. There was no popular demand for village elections. It has been argued that "progressive conservatives" like Peng feared the collapse of rural order following the dismantling of the commune system. Elections were seen as a way of placing party officials in control. Although he did talk of accountability of the party to the people, Peng himself saw no contradiction between strong state control and village democracy.

Officially, the claim is that direct elections to village committees have taken place in China's approximately 930,000 villages at least once since 1987. Independent scholars, however, estimate that this proportion is much less at between one-third and one-half. These elections have evoked world-wide interest and a number of foreign institutions like the Ford Foundation, Asia Foundation and the Carter Centre are involved in both monitoring and impact assessment. Five years ago, the law making village elections compulsory went through radical changes that introduced free nomination of candidates, secret voting, transparent ballot counting and the right to recall. Undoubtedly, the party is still paramount but gradually elected village committees are taking root in the

115

countryside. These committees comprise three to seven people elected to serve a term of three years and are overseen by a village representative assembly comprising all village residents. All administrative matters of the village, including tax collection, are entrusted to these committees.

Between 1997 and 2001, the issue of elections at higher levels became a subject of considerable controversy. Jiang Zemin made contradictory statements but Zhu Rongji clearly expressed his preference for direct township elections. While Beijing dithered, Lianjiang Li writing in the *China Quarterly* points out that some provinces "adopted the time-tested strategy of doing without asking". Thus, it was that Nancheng and Buyan townships in Sichuan province had direct elections in November and December 1998 respectively. Buyan hit the world headlines. Subsequently, direct township elections have taken place in Shanxi, Henan and Shenzhen provinces. Indeed, this "doing without asking" approach provided the backdrop to the 1987 village democracy law since in late 1980 and early 1981 a few villages in Guangxi province had simply gone ahead on their own and formed village committees.

It is most improbable that democracy in China will evolve along Indian lines—even Chinese champions of greater democracy in the mainland do not have such an agenda. The greatest fear of the modern-day Chinese intellectual elite and its emerging middle classes, is chaos. This mindset is born out of the trauma caused by the collapse of social order during the Cultural Revolution of 1966-69. The difference between Indian-style democracy and chaos to any observer outside India is thin. The dominant view is that the experience of Taiwan in the 1990s notwithstanding, democracy is simply not in the Chinese gene. Indeed, this was one of the themes of Samuel Huntington's influential *Clash of Civilisations* based on a selective reading of Confucianism. But with increasing globalisation and with the explosive growth of mobile telephony and the Internet (now around 120 million Netizens), civil society could well open up with unpredictable consequences. Globalisation is both strengthening Han nationalism (even though "Han" is a mixture of various ethnic groups) and creating space for western values, culture and consumption styles. Chinese rebels are neither extinct nor endangered. The community is growing as Ian Buruma describes in his recent *Bad Elements*, although as he himself recognises many of the protesters and dissidents are Christians.

In 2000 Jiang Zemin saw the need to broadbase the CCP and came up with his famous "three represents" theory to make the party more widely acceptable, particularly to the newly emerging entrepreneurial classes. How the Chinese deal with Hong Kong will reveal their intentions—according to the Basic Law that governs the city for fifty years after the Chinese takeover in 1997, direct elections are permitted after 2007. How the Chinese deal with increasing agitations of unemployed workers and frustrated farmers and with the backlash arising out of the dilution of the powers of provinces as the full impact of the WTO accession plays itself out will also be crucial.

Gathering Tempest?

The world sees India and China as huge
HIV/AIDS time bombs ticking away

China and India evoke images of (i) the world's two most populous countries; (ii) the world's two fastest growing economies soon that would occupy second and third position in world GDP rankings; and (iii) the destination of the world's blue collar and white collar jobs respectively. But the dynamic duo have also acquired a darker and more dubious reputation which they prefer not to talk about. The world health community sees China and India as potential HIV/AIDS time bombs waiting to explode in the next two-three decades.

Bill Clinton's recent sojourns brought the issue of HIV/AIDS in the two nations into global focus yet again. On November 10th at an AIDS Summit in Beijing, he called for stronger leadership to combat the spread of HIV/AIDS in China. On November 22nd in Delhi, he secured the involvement of three Indian companies - Ranbaxy, Cipla and Matrix - to supply cheap drugs for antiretroviral combination therapy for HIV/AIDS patients in Africa and the Caribbean.

There is no shortage of doomsday scenarios. While on a visit to Beijing the US Health Secretary Tommy Thompson said that the rapid spread of HIV/AIDS in India and China could destroy chances to contain or cure the disease. In November/December 2002, writing in the sober but prestigious US journal *Foreign Affairs,* Nick Eberstadt provided new ammunition. In 2002, China is estimated to have had about 0.85-1 million HIV/AIDS cases. Eberstadt estimates that by 2025, this could rise to between 32 million ("mild epidemic") and 100 million ("severe epidemic). The corresponding numbers for India range between 30 million and 140 million on a 2002 base of 3.8-4.6 million. By the end of 2000, Chinese government officials themselves now publicly talk of 10 million HIV/AIDS cases in the PRC. Indian government officials are more cautious in public but privately concede that India could also have 8-10 million HIV/AIDS cases by 2010. China is reporting an annual growth rate of 30%, while India's reported annual growth rate of HIV/AIDS cases in 2002 s was much lower at around 15%.

It is only since 2001 that the Chinese government has acknowledged HIV/AIDS to be a serious issue. In late 2001 the world media focused attention on the very high rates of HIV/AIDS prevalence in the central province of Henan. Henan is China's most populous province, apart from being Mao's home. The severe AIDS outbreak here was apparently caused by blood-buying companies using unclean methods. These methods have continued. Blood donations have become a widespread source of supplementing incomes in many parts of rural China. The breakdown of the rural commune-based health system over the past decade and a half and massive urban migrations appear to be contributing to the crisis.

Not surprisingly, provinces adjoining Henan such as Anhui, Heibei and Hubei are also suffering serious consequences. In other provinces like northwestern Xinjiang, HIV/AIDS has been spread on account of intravenous drug use. In provinces like Yunnan, Guangxi and Sichuan in the south and southeast, resurgence of prostitution is being seen as contributing significantly to the spread of HIV/AIDS. Yunnan is where the AIDS epidemic was first noticed and it is estimated that it accounts for almost half of all HIV/AIDS cases, although this could also be the result of better epidemiological monitoring. Just last month, Li Liming, Director of the Chinese office of the US Centre for Disease Prevention and Control revealed that almost two-third of HIV/AIDS patients were infected through intravenous drug use and about one-tenth each through unsafe plasma sales and sexual transmission.

India too was in denial mode for long. But since the mid-1990s, an active National AIDS Control Organisation (NACO) with its counterparts in states has come into being. Unlike the Chinese programme, India's programme is better organised and better funded. NACO has been spending close to $ 50 million a year and this could increase to around $ 80 million a year during 2004-2010. This excludes whatever financial support organisations like the Gates Foundation are expected to provide to NGOs directly. But even with the involvement of such organisations, NACO's investments will drive the country's programme.

India's investment in AIDS control may appear impressive in relation to the numbers for China which vary currently between $15-25 million a year. But clearly NACO is substantially under-funded. One casualty of the under-funding is anti-retroviral therapy which is not used by NACO since it costs around $1 per patient per year. Ironically, Indian companies are global leaders in anti-HIV/AIDS drugs. Other countries like Brazil, South, Botswana and now South Africa have made such therapy an integral element of their AIDS control efforts.

India's HIV/AIDS incidence has distinct regional variations with Andhra Pradesh, Karnataka, Maharashtra, Manipur, Nagaland and Tamil Nadu being the high-prevalent zone where epidemic levels may already have been reached, measured by HIV prevalence in antenatal women. Manipur and Nagaland suffer on account of intravenous drug use like in Xinjiang and Yunnan. That Manipur, Nagaland and Yunnan are close to Myanmar and Thailand has surely impacted on widespread drug use leading to high HIV/AIDS prevalence rates. India has also registered some successes. A very high rate of condom use in Sonagachi, for instance, is widely heralded as a major breakthrough for NACO, as has been the significant improvements in the blood supply chain all over the country. Political leadership has provided momentum to AIDS communication and control, especially in Andhra Pradesh and Tamil Nadu. It has also helped that India's most populous states are low HIV/AIDS prevalence zones, unlike the populous Chinese provinces. Whether this has to do with cultural practices or poor reporting or low urbanisation or because of low in-migration is difficult to tell. That low-prevalence must remain so since these poor, populous states have appalling health infrastructure unlike the peninsular states with high HIV/AIDS prevalence rates.

What about vaccines? Presently, a number of vaccines developed by various companies like AlphaVax, Chiron, Aventis Pasteur, GlaxoSmithKline, Merck, Therion, VaxGen and Wyeth are under different stages of clinical trials. VaxGen's human clinical trials in Thailand have just been announced to be a failure but hopes have not faded for making a safe and efficacious vaccine available in the market by the beginning or the middle of the next decade. Interestingly but not surprisingly, many of the top researchers in the US are scientists of Indian or Chinese origin. David Ho who discovered drug "cocktail" therapy is Taiwan-born and the head of Emory University's Vaccine Research Centre whose vaccine is under trial is headed by Hyderabad-born Rafi Ahmed. But neither India nor China can afford to sit back waiting for such a vaccine even while they participate in clinical trials themselves.

AIDS is no longer considered a health or a social or an economic issue. It is now being reckoned as a "security" issue. The UN Security Council and the UN General Assembly have both debated HIV/AIDS. The possibility of HIV/AIDS being used to check labour flows into the

West also cannot be ruled out. Both India and China face a stupendous challenge. They can and must cooperate in mounting an effective and credible response, learning from the success that one of their close partner countries—Thailand—has had in this area.

Hot Fudge In Beijing

All of a sudden, China is accused of
Enron-type manipulations

Is Jaswant Singh having the last laugh? On January 21, 2002 he created a stir while addressing an international audience in the capital when he said that China was "fudging" its growth numbers. Now, along come *The Economist* of the UK and *Newsweek* of the US with long articles that question China's national output, or GDP, statistics in particular.

It has generally been recognised that Chinese growth is exaggerated by at most 2 percentage points: that is, when the Chinese claim a 9 per cent rate of economic growth during 1978-97, it could well be 7 per cent, a great feat nevertheless considering that it is an annual compound rate of increase. But now there are far more serious accusations and the man to first give international respectability to these charges is an eminent American economist and China scholar, Thomas Rawski of the University of Pittsburgh. Since early 2000, Rawski has been writing extensively on the dubiousness of recent Chinese growth figures. He believes that the problems started in 1998 after the East Asian crisis, when, faced with the prospect of declining growth in exports and foreign investment, Chinese Prime Minister Zhu Rongji launched a personal crusade for an 8 per cent rate of economic growth terming it a "great political responsibility".

Shorn of all technical detail, what Rawski says is that China's reported GDP growth during 1998-2001:

● implies a drop in energy use and an increase in energy efficiency which is simply inconceivable;

● is based on an increase in farm output that could not have been realised given the extensive natural disasters that hit China in recent years;

● is not consistent with the sharp fall in investment spending and with the indifferent growth in retail sales.

Rawski's own estimates are that in 1998 and 1999, the Chinese economy may well have had a negative growth rate of around 2 per cent. In 2000, as against the official figure of 8 per cent, Rawski estimates a 2-3 per cent growth and in 2001, as against the 7.9 per cent claim, the alternative "realistic" estimate is 3-4 per cent. Interestingly, Rawski's doubts are based extensively on Chinese official, academic and media sources of criticism. The major culprit seems to be the data being generated by local and provincial governments. Chinese scholars have been writing about a "wave of deliberate falsification and embellishment", comparable to the harvest data during the disastrous Great Leap Forward in the late 1950s which hid 25-35 million famine deaths from the public for almost three decades.

However, in an e-mail, Nicolas Lardy, a distinguished American economist on China currently at Washington's Brookings Institution and author of the just released *Integrating China into the World Economy*, pointed out that:

- China's import growth in the past four years does not support the contention that the economy is contracting or sharply decelerating. This import data is consistent with export figures in trading partner countries like the US.

- Monetary growth has been substantial and if real output is falling as Rawski claims, this should have resulted in increasing inflation. This has not happened.

- If GDP growth is falling then family incomes should also be declining. But household savings have been growing, a sign of an expanding, not collapsing economy.

The debate will go on. Doomsday books like Gordon Chang's recent *The Coming Collapse of China* will continue to hit the stands. But what should not be missed is the tangible nature of Chinese growth. Poverty and backwardness still prevail widely but the spectacular pace of change is visibly evident. Visually, China's performance is simply awesome. Even our 8 per cent growth regions of Gujarat and Maharashtra or the Bangalores and Hyderabads do not come anywhere close to what can be seen in China. That is primarily because growth is being accompanied by massive urban renewal and frenzied construction activity, unlike in India. Further, China continues to extend its dominance in labour-intensive

127

mass manufacturing like consumer goods, toys, personal appliances and gadgets and textiles. It has also, with the help of Taiwanese firms, become the world's third largest power in IT hardware. "Made in China" is ubiquitous. This in any case is not new. Even during the Great Leap Forward, agricultural production figures were way over the real output and led to erroneous decisions when setting quotas for different regions. However, despite the problems of statistical accuracy, there is no denying that the Chinese economy is living up to its projection as one of the most successful economies of the world today.

Afterword

China-India has become a growth industry in the past two-three years. This is particularly true in the USA. The CIA has come out with a report that has hit the headlines. So have investment banks like Goldman Sachs and Morgan Stanley and Standard and Poors, the credit rating agency. The Woodrow Wilson Centre for International Scholars and the Asia Society have recently brought out a book with contributions by eminent political scientists, economists and strategic experts. The Harvard Business School has a programme on this subject. A growing number of scholars—not large enough as yet - in India and China are also engaging themselves in comparative analysis, even though the dominant tendency is to look at each other through works of American "experts". One former US ambassador to India would often assert, much to the delight of his Indian interlocutors, that the rise of China is a threat for both America and India.

In many ways, this current wave of interest harks back to the early 1950s when democratic India was juxtaposed against Communist China. That India did not see itself in a race against China was a minor irrelevancy. Indeed, India went out of its way to cultivate friendship with China, a friendship that enabled it to play a key role during the Korean conflict and during peace negotiations in Indo-China in the 1950s. Jawaharlal Nehru accorded the highest priority to building close ties with China at a time when it was being treated as a pariah by the US and most of Europe. But the world saw India and China pitted against each other and encouraged that "pitting" so to speak.

The wheel has come full circle. Once again, China and India are engaging the world's attention, not just singly but as a duo. There are profound differences between the two—in their history, in their ecology, in their political systems and in their social structures—that have influenced economic outcomes. This has not prevented the mushrooming of a minor industry built around a comparative *evaluation* of India and China. I have always felt that it is more meaningful to speak of the comparative *evolution* of India and China since both are *sui generis* in their own complex ways. This anthology is a modest contribution to this end.